The Ginger Italian Stories

George Zito

To my amazing family, my wife and two children you are my magic and wonder.

This book is about the loss and grief of people past and present. Big love to all the family who I never got to meet.

Contents

1. Nonno Page 5
2. Funky Angel Page 91
3. Alfred Lemon Page 142
4. Cat Agency Page 166
5. The Screwdriver Brothers Page 182
6. Swim with the Fishes Page 215
7. The Adventures of Danny and Uncle Phil the Space Pirate Page 230

Nonno

1900 Caserta, Italy.

In a village called Grazzanise, Caserta Naples lived a boy called Stefano Russo. He was twelve years old and lived with his Mother Laura, his father Paolo and his younger brother Pasquale who was five years old.

Southern Italy in 1900, was a time of severe poverty and hardship for ordinary people. Families shared rooms with many other relatives and cousins. Their flat was in a run-down block of rooms. The plaster on the building was peeling, with huge holes where the plaster had crumbled. As you entered the entrance paint was peeling off the ceilings. The stench of so many families crammed into tiny spaces, with a lack of hygiene and clean water. Many families got cholera or people died from simple wounds, that would turn into septicaemia. Italy was a recently unified country but had a very large debt, very few natural resources, and no transportation or industries.

Southern Italy was in bad condition. More than half of the inhabitants in the area were still illiterate. These areas had problems with absentee landlords, rebellion, organized crime, and even starvation. Thousands of Southern Italians were leaving the new nation of Italy every year during this time, hoping for a better life in America. Poverty alongside organised crime with local officials and thieving landlords had plagued fear on the Southern Italians.

As the cockerel crowed loudly, Stefano woke up and threw his clothes on. He ran out of the apartment and down the dry track to his friend Nick's home. Stefano called for Nick outside the wooden door to his home. They both left and ran to the farm.

They were both going to help Stefano's Uncle Raffael, who ran a farm with orchards of fruit and olive trees.

Both young men liked helping Uncle Rafael, he was a kind man and loved his animals and kept bees to make honey.

Uncle Raffael had a son the same age as Stefano called Alberto.

The smell of manure got stronger as they approached Uncle Rafael's farm. They took a shortcut through the tobacco fields; they were not far from their uncle's home. They could hear shouting; they stopped in the tobacco fields. They were frightened by the shouting and hid behind the long plants. They saw two men with guns, Rafael tried to push Alberto away from the men. He then charged at the men, and our aunty Maria went to grab the gun from the man. A shot was fired, followed by four more shots. The men looked around and then left quickly on their horses.

Stefano and Nick were breathing heavily and overwhelmed with fear.

Stefano said,

"I am so frightened, let's get home before they kill our families."

Nick just nodded and they both tried to run, but their legs felt like heavy weights. They had to keep stopping, to catch their breath and wipe their tears away.

Nick banged on his door,

“Papa open!”

Stefano ran to his home and banged on his door, he was crying,

“Mama, Papa, it’s Uncle Raffael and Maria, Alberto has been shot. Quick, we need help!”

Paolo got to the door and saw his son crying. Paolo cuddled his son,

” What has happened Stefano?”

Stefano repeated what he had said.

Paolo’s face changed, his face filled with anger and rage. Stefano had never seen his father face turn to hate and bright red with anger.

“Stay here son, stay here. I am going to round up some men and go over.”

Stefano was so scared,

“Please father, don’t go. I do not want you to get hurt.”

Paolo cuddled his son and went to gather the men from the village.

Paolo, Nick's father Roberto and eight other men saddled their horses, horse, and carts. They charged ahead like an army going into battle. The dry earth rose and clouded like storms in a desert, as the horses and men sped off into the hazy heat.

Stefano and Nick were still upset and crying at what they had witnessed. The mums were wailing and crying too. Laura and Nick's Mother Angela just hugged their children and wept in pain.

Angela's daughter Nicolina was two years younger than her brother Nick. She just hugged her mum, frozen in time, staring at all her family in their grief.

When the men came back the children were sent inside. The men had bought Raphael, Maria's and Alberto's bodies on their horse and cart. The bodies were covered with brown woollen blankets.

Paolo went over to his wife and hugged her. Tears just flowed down his face.

His voice was croaky as he muttered,

"Revenge and death to those criminals who did this. I swear I will make it my life ambition to get them."

One of the men went to get the priest. The priest came, and he was horrified at the tragic loss of this family. He read the last rights and blessed each body with Holy Water.

The men had to carry the bodies by horse and cart to the local cemetery. Because of the heat, they had to bury the bodies straight away. All the men removed their hats in respect to Raphael's family. They buried their family and life stood still, frozen in trauma and pain.

Raphael's land now belonged to a rich landlord, the boss of an organised crime gang. To get justice meant taking the law into your own hands. The trauma of what Paolo and the other men saw of Raphael, Maria, and Antonio will stay with them forever.

Grazzanise 1909- Stefano 21 Years Old

Stefano tossed and turned in his sleep, drenched with sweat from the heat of the night.

Shouting, "No, no!"

His body jerked and he sat up upright, stunned by his nightmares.

Stefano's mother Laura was at the end of his bed, waiting patiently with a cup of espresso coffee. She passed him a cloth to wipe his face, then she passed the coffee. Steam from the coffee could be seen rising from the cup.

Stefano was twenty-one years old. He was of stocky build, with dark curly hair, and a moustache. He shared their home, with his father Paolo and his twelve-year-old brother Pasquale. His father was snoring in the corner of the room, and his brother was deep asleep.

Laura reassured her son Stefano and he sat on the edge of the bed, still shocked by his nightmare. She comforted her son, as tears fell down her cheeks. She tried to quickly wipe the tears away, to not show that she was upset.

They both stayed up talking until the cockerel sounded the alarm call.

The room was cramped with all the makeshift beds at the end of the room. There was a small stove to heat up the room and cook with.

As they all got up early at five in the morning, Laura had put the coffee pot on for expresso coffee. Pasquale had to give up school so that he could help his family on the land. They all had a coffee.

They left the house at five-thirty in the morning. The sun had already risen. The three men were wearing their flat caps and their only set of work clothes. Each member of Stefano's family had boots with holes in their soles. They would all use old leather or paper to wear as insoles in the shoes.

They walked through Grazzinissi village, all men, women, and children were all leaving to work on the land.

They would all meet and walk the dry paths, with their fissures in the soil, from the hot sun and the walnut trees lining the way ahead.

Later that morning his mother Laura would come to help on the land. To survive you had to do back-breaking work. Both men and women had to work on the land to survive. Women brought their children as they worked in the intense hot sun. The little money they earned barely fed the family.

Stefano was in love with his childhood sweetheart called Nicolina. He loved her so much that he wanted her to be his wife. It was traditional for his best friend to ask Nicolina's parents if Stefano could marry their daughter. His best friend just happened to be Nicolina's brother called Nick.

Nick was also twenty-one with red hair and fair skin. He was often made fun of, due to his fair looks and red hair.

As they were working, Stefano stopped to drink some water. He threw the bottle of water at Nick. Stefano smiled,

"Hey, best friend. I need you to do a big favour?"

Nick smiled,

"You want me to ask my parents if you can marry Nicolina? It's about time, we have been waiting for you to ask for several years. You know my mother has been putting bedding, towels, and baby clothes in her bottom drawer for years."

Stefano jokingly punched Nick in the arm.

"I have been worrying about asking you, for a year, just in case you were going to be angry with me."

"We couldn't ask for a better husband for my sister. You know you will have to go and serenade my sister."

Stefano looked uncomfortable,

"She won't marry me for my singing?"

Nick patted him on the back,

"It's tradition, my parents will expect you to sing, for her hand in marriage."

Stefano and Nick went back to work on the land harvesting the olives. It was hard work in the blistering heat.

Nick found the work in this intense heat difficult, he made sure he took breaks under the shade of one of the olive trees. Stefano would always help Nick get his quota, as they got paid on the weight of olives picked.

Stefano's and Nick's Mothers also worked on the land picking tobacco leaves. This was also back-breaking work, as the women picked the leaves and put a thin metal rod through the leaves, so they could be dried out.

At two pm, the sun was at its warmest, bright orange and intense heat. Stefano and Nick were sweating, their clothes were drenched with sweat. It was time to stop for a siesta. Nick shared his water bottle with Stefano.

Nick smiled,

"I can't wait to tell my parents that you want to marry Nicolina. You are going to be my brother-in-law."

"You know I love your sister, with all my heart. When I see Nicolina, I can't get my words out. I feel magical when I am with her. I mean it Nick; she means the world to me."

Proposal

Marriage comes at a cost. It was customary for the bride's family to pay the costs of the wedding. In this small village, word already had got to Father Assunto. He decided to call Nicolina's home, to discuss if the rumour was true of their intended marriage to Stefano. It was customary to feed the priest if he visited.

Father Assunto found the rumour to be true and advised that Stefano and Nicolina would have to visit him, before getting married. This was to talk about the wedding vowels and discuss the gift of having children. Then casually he named a price in Lira to the family. They were all struggling financially, and Nicolina's father Marco looked worried at the cost.

"Father, we work all day in the hot sun to survive. This kind of money is not available, it is going to take a while to save this."

Father Assunto listened, he said, "Your money will be invested in God your daughter, your son-in-law and your future grandchildren."

He sat down. He was a portly man and made sure he got fed with his pasta and scraps of meat. As soon as he finished his food, he got up and blessed the house, and left.

That evening Stefano saw Nicolina's parents walking together. He went over to them to say hello. They looked like they had the whole world on their shoulders.

Nicolina's father Carmen said,

"We are so proud to hear that you and Nicolina want to get married. Father Assunto came over yesterday and told us how much we must pay the church, for you both to get married. We are struggling and feeling under pressure, to get this kind of money."

Stefano smiled "Carmen, it's okay I can help. I have been saving for this day for many years. Please let me help you. I don't want you to feel embarrassed or sad. No one will know that I have given you the money."

Stefano went home and got his hidden tin from under the floorboards. The tin was worn and old with red and blue paint on it. The lid to the tin was very stiff, Stefano prized it open. Inside were a lot of Lira notes. He closed the lid and wrapped the tin in a cloth. He left his home and went over to Nicolina's home. He knocked on the door and was invited in by Nicolina's mother Maria.

He handed the tin to Carmen.

"We are all going to be one family, what's mine is yours."

Carmen looked sad taking the tin and shook Stefano's hand.

"Thank you, Stefano. You are a good man. We can't take your money. It makes me look disrespectful. People will think I can't even afford my own daughter's wedding."

"I know what proud people you are, but times are hard. Everyone is just surviving. Please take the money, I love your daughter and this makes me feel proud I can help my family."

Carmen took the tin and counted the money for the priest. There was some leftover and he wanted to get them both a present.

Stefano was a chatty and lively person; he was well-liked by all the local people in his village. Like so many people in his village, his wife would have to live with Stefano and his family in their one-room flat.

There were no toilets or washing facilities. The toilet and makeshift shower were in the field, the shower near the well. Everything was done near the well, from washing clothes and scrubbing them with a stone.

The cesspit for a toilet was across the field away from the well, there was a makeshift seat and when the pit was full, they buried the waste and made another pit away from the well.

Stefano wanted a better life for Nicolina and his future family.

On one sunny Sunday afternoon, Stefano and Nicolina were allowed to go for a walk together to the Royal Palace of Caserta, chaperoned by Nick.

Once they were at the palace, Nick gave them some privacy. Stefano kissed Nicolina once they were outside the palace grounds.

He asked her,

“If she could have one wish, what would it be?”

She smiled,

“I just want our own home together and a better life for our children.”

Stefano nodded,

“The only way to improve our money situation was to go to New York. What if Nick and I went, and earned the money to buy our house?

Nicolina cuddled Stefano.

“I would miss you so much. How long would you go for?

Stefano gazed into her eyes,

"I would miss you too. I suppose I would go for a year or two, but I am not sure."

Nicolina and Stefano held hands and slowly walked around the edge of the palace. They took in the opulence and grandeur of this beautiful palace. Before they left to walk home, Nicolina stopped Stefano.

"I don't see any other way out of poverty. You see my parents want to get us a wedding present, what if they bought you and Nick tickets to sail to New York?"

Stefano looked at Nicolina,

"Do you think we should do this? We would not see each other for a while? Plus, your parents could use that money for your family."

Nicolina kissed Stefano on his lips,

"They want to make our lives better than theirs. If we do nothing, we will just be poor forever."

They left the palace and walked hand in hand, with Nick just behind them.

Wedding

Over the weeks Nicolina's mum Maria had saved her wedding dress for her daughter. It was a beautiful lace neck and silk body; with tiny sparkling sequins down the dress. The dress needed some adjustments, her aunts, and cousins all wanted to help tailor this elegant dress. They worked in secret day and night, to get the dress ready.

The Wedding Day was set for Wednesday 10th February 1909, at the Catholic Church of St. Paolina Capua. Stefano picked Nick to be his best man. Nick had got Stefano up early that morning, to prepare him for the big day. They both woke up and had a coffee and a shot of Strega each.

Stefano had one good suit, he dusted it off. He got dressed and brushed his hair.

Nick asked a friend if they could pick them both up in their horse and cart from home to the church, then go and pick up his sister and family.

The horse and cart arrived; the cart was decorated in white braided material.

Stefano and Nick climbed into the cart and sped off to the church. They got there early. Stefano and Nick had to wait outside. The Priest got his volunteers from the village to organise the flowers in the church. Stefano checked with Nick, that he had the rings. Stefano was extremely nervous and started to pace up and down. This was an old church; its décor needed refurbishments and a coat of paint. Some of the windows were missing the stained-glass panels. Stefano kept turning towards the door, then looking back at Nick. Then Families, relatives, and friends started to fill the church until it became full.

The entrance to the church had poor lighting, and then Stefano saw a bright white light at the door entrance. As the sunshine came streaming in. It was Nicolina in her beautiful lace and silk wedding dress. She was holding her father's arm and carrying a bouquet, while her mother fussed around the trail of the dress.

Stefano nearly fainted at the beauty of his wife-to-be. Nick moved next to Stefano to prop him up.

Stefano's young brother Pasquale sat at the front of the church with his Mum and Dad. Stefano winked at Pasquale.

Nicolina's mother arranged her daughter's dress, while Nicolina linked her father's arm. Nick and Pasquale patted Stefano on his back. Stefano was frozen in his gaze, as he saw the beauty of his wife-to-be.

As the Altar boys sang, the bride and her father walked slowly up the aisle to the altar.

Nicolina illuminated the whole church, in her beautiful white wedding dress. The priest greeted both families. Both Mothers started crying, you could hear them blowing their noses. The priest read the wedding vows, as Stefano looked into Nicolina's eyes. Nick handed both rings to the Priest.

The Priest had read the vows and made the sign of the cross.

"In the name of the Father, Son, and Holy Ghost. He had pronounced them man and wife."

Pasquale shouted out,

" Kiss then."

Stefano held Nicolina gently, he lifted her veil and kissed his wife.

Nicolina and Stefano led the procession out of the church. Outside the whole village came to pay their respects. Tables were put out in the street, near the church.

Everyone contributed food and wine to the wedding. As they all sat, Stefano's mother started tapping on her glass, with her fork,

"Kiss, kiss."

They kissed and everyone started clapping.

Stefano's family came over to Nicolina's family and they all hugged and congratulated each other. Stefano, Nicolina, Nick, and their families were at the top table.

Nicolina asked her brother Nick to give her the present to Stefano. She gently passed her husband the envelope. Stefano carefully opened it and there was a ticket for New York. Stefano was shocked, he held up the ticket.

"A ticket to New York. The ticket says to leave Naples, Friday 26th March 1909."

Nicolina kissed Stefano,

"If you go to New York, make us enough money to buy our own home. No more struggling for our family and future bambinos. Nick is going with you. The ticket cost my family, thirty-five dollars each. I will miss you, my husband. But this is our way out of poverty."

Everyone clapped at the gift of going to New York. Stefano felt anxious and looked at his new wife.

"I have one month with my wife; I don't know what America has to offer. I know you are right, the only way out of poverty. It just feels difficult as we have just got married and I will miss my lovely wife and family."

Nick put his arm around Stefano.

"We can do this together and come back richer men."

Pasquale, Stefano's younger brother came over.

"Wow, you are going to America, can I come with you?"

Stefano put his arm around his young brother,

"You are too young, but you will get your chance to travel when you are older."

Naples, Italy 26th March 1909.

Stefano and his brother-in-law Nick, were waiting to board the Prinzess Irene passenger liner, to New York America. The sun's horizon filled the sky and its rays glistened in the calm Naples Sea. Stefano held his wife's hand tightly. They could only afford a one-way, third-class ticket. Stefano looked back at his home town Napoli, with sadness in his heart. He felt alone for the first time. But he had to do something to end their family's struggle with poverty, it was time to make a better life.

Many people and families were queuing for the hope of new dreams and adventures. People were leaving poverty, corruption, and crime, in the hope of opportunity and a better life. Every person handed in their paperwork to be processed, as the ordinary people queued patiently for the third-class quarter. It was hard to get the paperwork completed as most people queuing were illiterate.

Prinzess Irene was a huge steamship, with two giant black funnels, docked in the port of Naples. Stefano, Nick, and Nicolina could not believe the size of the liner. Stefano and Nick's family all came to see them off. Both men hugged their families and Stefano hugged and kissed his wife, Nicolina. He did not know when he would see her again. Nicolina said it twice.

"You will get your home, my love, I love you with all my heart."

"You will get your home; I love you with all my heart."

Stefano hugged Nicolina again, tender and kissed her. Nicolina cried and was emotionally upset; she handed her husband a food parcel.

"Love you so much."

Stefano and Nick waved at their families as they moved up the queue on the creaky gangplank to the ship. They were quiet with their thoughts about their adventures ahead.

Stefano said to Nick,

"I hope we are doing the right thing. I am going to miss Nicolina so much."

Nick nodded,

"They say anything is possible in America and dreams can come true."

As they shuffled along the gangplank, there were so many families and people queuing, with all their possessions. With dreams of a better place out of poverty, to the land of milk and honey.

As they boarded Prinzess Irene, this was a huge steam passenger liner with two large black funnels. Both young men now entered the third-class deck. They both had one glance back at their homeland.

They showed their tickets and carried their small case each on board the ship. The ship's crew wrote their names, ages, and the area they came from in their passenger log book. They put tags on their cases and stamped their passports.

The two crew members pointed for directions to the third-class quarters.

One of the crew said,

“Can you save the bunk beds for families, there will be blankets for adults so that can sleep on the floor.”

Rows of bunk beds filled the quarters of the third class, but not enough for everyone travelling. The tables were crate boxes, also the empty crate boxes were doubled up as chairs. So many of the families grabbed the beds and basic mattresses. Families with several children, newborn babies.

There was so much noise with all the families and people coming to the third-class deck. Stefano and Nick grabbed a blanket each and moved to the side of the deck. Babies were crying and men were arguing over getting beds for their families.

The two men watched while all the families took all the bunks. It was noisy, as excited families, children, and babies settled into their new home of hope.

Babies were crying, and children playing and running around. Parents shouting at each other, worried at what lies ahead.

Stefano and Nick sat around one of the crates and started playing cards. They both lit a cigarette and just focused on the cards.

Stefano looked up to see a young man on his own, he looked lost in all the people. Stefano gestured to the man to come over.

"Come over and sit with us."

The man came over and shook hands with Stefano and Nick.

"My name's Antonio, I'm from Genoa. I can't believe how many people are going to New York."

Nick gestured with his hands,

"We are all chasing dreams for a better life."

Antonio smiled,

"Me too. Although, I have heard a lot of stories about gangs and having to pay protection money."

Stefano nodded,

"Let's just take one day at a time."

The ship sounded her horn and announced their departure to New York.

12 Day Voyage

The three men Stefano, Nick and Antonio sat around the crate table, as the ship eased herself out of the calm seas of Naples docks. They were playing cards, with their only possessions in their small cases near the table. Nick got salami out of his case; he used his penknife to cut some off for the other two. Stefano counted the matches and dealt the cards to the other two men. Kids were chasing each other across the deck. A couple of kids came over, to watch the game. Stefano added the matches to the stakes. As the game developed, each would raise the stakes with matches. Nick raised the stakes and Antonio matched the stakes. The two lads watching were about ten years old. They pulled up crate boxes and sat close to their table. They were both sitting on the edge of their boxes, excited by the game and trying to guess what cards the men had.

Stefano raised the stakes again; Nick matched the stakes. Antonio looked at his cards and threw his cards to the table.

Nick raised the stakes. Stefano picked up a card and matched the stakes. Nick laid his cards down and went to pull in the matches. Stefano stopped his hand from going near the matches and laid his hand down.

He then scooped all the matches in his direction. Nick waved his arms in the air, in disbelief. The two young kids cheered for Stefano.

There was a kitchen area to prepare food. Stefano and Nick had used a wooden crate box, as a table and entertainment playing cards. Young children would come over and watch them play cards. Stefano and Nick would teach the kids the card game. Antonio showed them card tricks.

The men snacked on dry bread and bits of salami.

Stefano said,

"Shall we all go and have a look around."

Antonio and Nick nodded.

They all got up Nick said to the young lads,

"If you watch our cases, I will teach you to play cards."

The two lads agreed and stayed sitting on the wooden crates.

The Cafe

"You guys want a coffee?"

Antonio said,

"We don't have a lot of money, Antonio. There was a kitchen area where we can make food."

Antonio said,

"It's okay, I have got some money."

They left the third class and made their way to the second-class floor. The café sold coffee, soft drinks, alcohol, snacks and pastries, and tobacco. As they entered the café Stefano noticed three men in the corner, giving them a stare.

Antonio asked the guys,

"What do you fancy?

Stefano,

"Just expresso."

Nick said,

"Same, thanks, Antonio."

Antonio ordered a pastry and expresso and handed the Café Attendant a five-dollar bill.

This caught the eyes of the three men in the corner, looking like Hawkes. Their eyes lit up as they saw Antonio hand the money to the café manager.

Stefano knew the men were looking over. Antonio paid and they sat and enjoyed the pastry and coffee. Stefano and Nick felt uncomfortable about the three people in the corner. The three men in the corner, got up to leave. One of those men stopped and said to Antonio,

"Does it taste good? You ought to be careful, carrying that kind of money around."

Antonio looked on as the man smiled touched the peak of his cap and left.

Stefano felt these three men could be trouble.

"Listen, we appreciate your generosity. But you got to be careful pulling money out. I think those wise guys might be part of the Black Hand Gang. We will need to stick together and watch ourselves"

That night Stefano had fallen asleep on the chair, Nick and Antonio lay on the floor with grey woollen itchy blankets over them. Stefano heard a creak in the floorboards. Without hesitation, he got up and pulled a knife from his jacket. It was those three men from the café, trying to sneak up on Antonio. Stefano nudged Nick with his foot. All the men sprang up.

Stefano grabbed the man at the front and held the knife to him. The other two men panicked. Stefano grabbed the man tight and put his knife to the man's throat.

One of the men said,

"If you hurt him, we will make sure none of you makes it alive to New York."

Stefano pushed the man over their table, this woke up families in their bunk beds.

Those three men crawled off. Antonio thanked his friends,

"You saved my life; I am indebted to you."

Stefano put his arm around Antonio, amigo. That means we all help each other out. You and Nick are my family now, what is mine is yours."

Antonio shook both Stefano's and Nick's hands.

"I am very lucky to meet true friends. I apologise if I would have been more discreet, they would not have attacked us?"

Nick turned to Antonio.

"These guys are part of the Black Hand Gang. They don't care whom they get their money from. They take from their poor people. I am not going to put up with bullies. Once you give in to them, they will be on your case all the time."

"Do you think we will have problems with them in New York?" said Antonio.

Stefano nodded,

"We need to keep our eyes open. We will meet others with whom we can connect with. Safety in numbers. Those wise guys will have their contacts and boss, who calls the shots."

After the incident, the men kept a watchful eye. They never went to another part of the deck by themselves and did not want to encourage revenge attacks on the boat or in New York. They played cards as normal and took turns sleeping in the afternoon and at night time.

Antonio noticed parents going without food to feed their families. These families had nothing and risked the journey for all their savings. Antonio decided he could not see families go hungry and where possible; he would buy food for the parents.

Antonio, Stefano, and Nick got to know a lot of people on the third-class deck. For several nights there were storms and rough seas. There were a lot of people feeling sick.

They saw those wise guys on our deck and around, doing their dirty business. They were using fear to threaten families and collect protection money. Stefano and Nick were helping a family from their village.

The man told them that

He had to pay three men. or there would be big trouble. He told us if we did not pay, he could not say what would happen to us in New York.

Stefano asked the man.

“Do you want us to sort this out for you?

He nodded and felt ashamed.

“I can’t afford to pay these men, but I don’t want to bring any trouble to my family.”

Stefano smiled.

“We are all paesano’s, you part of my family. Let’s stick together.”

He did not want to let this family down. The three men went back to their table. As they played cards, they discussed what they were going to do about these wise guys.

Antonio smiled,

"Should we shame them, for stealing from poor people?"

Stefano shook his head from side to side.

"These guys don't understand values. But if we turn them in, they will be deported. But we will be targets in New York. If we confront them, then we will be targets anyway."

Nick slammed his hand on the table.

"We need to tackle these diablos head-on! We will wait for them to come and do their rounds. Once they approach our friends, we will circle them."

Antonio said,

"I will buy some wood from a guy I know, who is working in the boiler room. We can make the wood into batons."

Antonio asked the furnace stokers for some wood-shaped batons. Later that night Antonio went down to the furnace areas and picked up the eight batons. He took them inside his coat and then hid them in their friend's bunk, under his mattress.

Stefano and Nick were keen to strike before those three men caused problems on their deck.

"What if we get everyone to stand up to them, let's be strong in numbers," said Antonio.

Stefano nodded,

"Good idea."

They went around all the men in the third class and encouraged the men to stand up to these bullies, or they would be indebted to them forever

The next day all the batons were given to those who could handle themselves. The three men in dark suits arrived at the third-class living quarters. Stefano, Antonio, and Nick were armed and ready.

As soon as the three men went over to the family man, to get their dirty money. They found themselves surrounded by most of the men on that deck. The three men were shocked and taken aback. Stefano was the first to strike one of the wise guys, this led to the group of men standing up to the three men. There was a lot of noise and shouting. This led some of the ship's crew to come down to investigate the commotion. The three men quickly hobbled off and left the deck, injured and bleeding. This sent a strong message and ended any racketeering from those men. Stefano, Nick, and Antonio looked after their people, they had to keep a lookout as they knew they would want revenge.

New York, New York

On the eleventh day, we could see the Statue of Liberty. All three men danced around each other, excited and hugging each other, like they had just discovered America. Antonio pointed at the Statue of Liberty,

"This is our freedom and escape from poverty."

The three men jumped around, dancing with other families on the third-class deck. All the families pointed to the Statue of Liberty; their children waved at the lady holding the torch of freedom.

When they got to Ellis Island the first class went first, then the second and then the third class. They were all documented and checked by the doctor. People with tuberculosis or other diseases had to go into quarantine. A lot of the third-class people were illiterate and did not know their date of birth, or how to spell their names. So, a lot of people were processed with incorrect details.

After all the documentation, the three men were asked to go outside, with their cases. Here employers came to recruit labour. Stefano knew that they should ask other men if they want to share a room to save money. He got ten men together whom he had met in the third class.

One of the employers was building a subway for trains to help people get around New York. The work in the subways was perilous and strenuous fourteen-hour shifts under damp, dark and dangerous conditions. So many labourers had died on this work. The three men were unaware of the work ahead.

The employer of the subways picked ten men by pointing his cane at them from his lavish carriage. His Italian workers came over to the men to tell them they were employed now and belonged to this gentleman. The man translated that they can live in a rented room, and money will be deducted from their pay, from the employer.

The ten men went with one of the landlords to Mulberry Street north of the Five Points, in Greenwich Village, and East Harlem, to their accommodation. There were lots of Italians living in the cramped accommodations and buildings. The room had basic mattresses on the floor, a blanket, a single toilet, and a washroom.

Everyone was so excited; we did not sleep on the first night. We all ventured out into the new land. Antonio treated us to some vegetables and fruit. The man who had the greengrocery shop was from Naples. He told Stefano, Nick, and Antonio about how Italians were treated like rats here in the land of milk and honey. He told them that their wages will be lower than anybody else's. He said he feared the Black hand gang; they ruled the roost here. We pay the gang to protect us from the locals as they don't like our ways, food, or culture. They keep trying to make us talk like them and attend their Christian churches.

Stefano let the man in the grocery shop know that he was starting work on the subway.

The grocery man warned Stefano,

“This is dangerous work. The pay is low and people die down there.”

Stefano, Antonio, and Nick shook the man’s hand in the shop and made their way through the busy streets of New York. The three men felt uneasy like they could be attacked.

Stefano said,

“Let’s keep together.”

They went back to the room where most of the men were sleeping. Most of the men in the room were illiterate. Those that could write a little started to write letters for other men to families in Italy, to tell them they had arrived safely.

The Subway

That morning the subway manager sent his men to meet his new labourers in the Bronx, Queens. They were taken to the start of a new subway construction at Queens. they were sent into a tunnel to dig the rubble and rocks, without any safety protection. It was back-breaking work, there was a water barrel where they could get a drink, outside of the tunnel. But if you kept getting a drink it was docked off your pay.

Stefano, Nick, and Antonio worked hard on their first day, they made friends with two new friends from Foggia Nicola Santo and Barto Luigi.

All the Italian men were living in cramped and poor accommodations on Mulberry Street north of the Five Points, in Greenwich Village, and East Harlem. Over weeks, of hard physical labour in dangerous conditions. They received their hard-earned wages.

Stefano looked at his salary,

"How are we meant to survive on this? They promised us that we would get paid the same as everyone else."

Nicola and Barto agreed. Nicola demanded to see the manager,

"I need to see the manager now!"

The person giving the wages shouted out of the office,

"Boss, these dagos are hollering and moaning about the wages we are paying them."

The manager came out of his room and spat tobacco at their feet.

"Because you are scum dagos. Scum on my shoe, boy! Looks like we got a troublemaker, get out of line, you are going back on that greasy boat, with the rest of the rats. You are lucky we pay you at all."

"We don't want more money; we just want to be paid the same as everyone else."

The manager stepped forward into Nicola's space and spat on his shoe.

"You Iti's are rat-infested scum, with your weird religion and food. Go back home dago, go back home to your rat holes. Your cards are marked if you think we tolerate troublemakers. Your life is a worthless rat, so get back to work before I beat you to death."

Stefano, Antonio, Nick, and Barto all stepped forward towards the manager. He stepped back, pulled a revolver, and shot it in the air.

Everyone moved back, the manager pointed the gun at Nicola.

"Move one step and I will blow your head off."

As the weeks went by all the Italians were sent into the most dangerous areas of the subway.

Two days later, one of the men from the room was digging in the subway and the tunnel collapsed.

All the men working in this area died. Stefano, gathered all the men from their room to help Nicola and Barto to try and rescue any survivors. But it was too late. All the men were in shock and grieving. Everyone was worried that they would die doing this work and their families would starve in Italy.

Nicola and Barto were both literate Italians and asked the manager for the men who died if they could send their wages and compensation back to their families in Italy.

The manager spat tobacco at him and then grabbed him by the lapels. Stefano stepped in.

"Get yourself out of here and back to your rat-infested country. If your other greasy Wop comes near me, you will be punished in prison."

Nicola pushed Stefano away and just stared at the manager, in disgust.

"We are not animals, we are people. Hardworking people."

The manager just spat on the floor and walked away.

"Until you lose your spic, greasy ways and attend the proper church, speak like us, then you will always be a greasy rat."

American people hate the Italians, they all thought they were involved in crime and up to no good. The elite tried to get the Italians to change their religion to a non-Catholic religion. They did not want them to celebrate their saint's days. The Italians refused to change their religion or food. They even had to attend separate Catholic churches to the Irish immigrants.

Nicola and Barto over the weeks knew that this work was too dangerous and used their contacts to get all ten men a job on the docks.

Docks of New York

Nicola and Barto knew some guys on the docks and they got Stefano, Nick, and Antonio all jobs. It was tough work with benefits. As shipments of goods and clothing came in, men would take some food to feed themselves and clothes to sell or send home. Nicolo and Barto joined the union and became officials to support all the Italian workers.

Stefano, Nick, and Antonio enjoyed their new job, they were working with many other Italians. Loading and unloading big cargo ships, working twelve to fourteen-hour shifts.

This new job gave the men some added income and a chance to get some luxury items. Everything from food to clothing. Stefano would send dresses and food to Nicolina. The men would sell the items at markets and through their contacts. This additional income made life more bearable. No one liked the Italians and this income meant they could eat better and afford clothes.

Stefano and Nick also sent money home to help their families. They soon made many more contacts and were selling their knocked-off goods to all the Italian restaurants, businesses, and shops. They helped their friend in the fruit and vegetable shop, with food imports.

Over the month Nick met an Italian girl called Maria Dovina; they fell in love. Later Nick found out that her real name was Maria Carlucci, sister of notorious gangster boss Vito Carlucci. She had to change her name to get into the country. Nick was in love and wanted to marry Maria but Stefano was uneasy about her family and getting involved with mobsters. This caused lots of arguments and Nick could not understand his brother-in-law's views and opinions.

Nicola and Barto had become union officials. They were making a name for themselves and fighting for the rights of Italian workers and pay. This caused pure hatred of the Italians by their bosses. But the union became so strong, that every Italian on the dock paid to be in this union.

When Nicola and Barto challenged the bosses, he got all the Italian men to down tools and follow them to the company's office. They managed to get all the workers a small pay rise. This caused a deeper hatred and these two men were now risking their lives as they had become targets against companies, by fighting for workers' rights and pay.

The big boss on the docks wanted Italians to attend their Christian church and try to stop the Italians from speaking their language and selling their food. In those desperate times, it was easy to understand why people got involved in organised crime. All the workers were poor and working long hours, for very little pay. They all just wanted enough food in their bellies, and a roof over their heads. They hated Italians, they didn't like their culture, religion, or food. All the Italians were put mostly in emigrant quarters, getting its name Little Italy. All the Italians helped each other in their community. Often, Stefano, Nick and Antonio would help their friend Luigi in the supermarket. Stefano would bring Luigi extra meat from the docks, for his family.

One day they went into the supermarket. Their friend looked pale; his hands were shaking.

“What’s up Luigi,” asked Stefano.

Luigi just nodded. Stefano got him a drink of water. Their friend sat down and looked terrified.

Luigi said,

“It was the Black Hand Gang; they want us to pay protection money or else.”

Nick said,

“How much do they want you to pay?”

Luigi swallowed and took a breath,

“Forty dollars a week. My boss won’t understand, he will think I’m stealing money from the till. If I don’t pay, they said I will be swimming with the fishes.”

Stefano looked concerned,

We can't let these bullies do this to our friends. I know these bullies are armed and part of a gang."

Antonio looked uneasy,

"We could get killed."

"We can't let our friend down Antonio."

They all agreed and went back into the shop. Stefano comforted the shopkeeper.

"We are here for you, when are the men coming for their money?"

The shopkeeper looked worried.

"I am thankful Stefano, but these men are dangerous, what if something happens to you, Nick, and Antonio? Is there going to be a shootout in the shop?"

Nick reassured the man,

“There won’t be a shootout. I got an idea to make sure all of us from our room are here. We will feel safer in numbers, we will embarrass them for stealing from their own.”

Stefano smiled,

“We will make them a deal and maybe we have to negotiate to give them free groceries instead?”

The three men went back to the flat. Stefano gathered everyone around and explained what was happening with their shopkeeper friend. All the men were in and willing to help their Luigi.

Stefano went to see Nicolo and Barto to see if they knew the boss of these mobsters.

Nicolo knew the boss.

“Let me talk to their boss, first.”

Both men knew the boss of this gang. They went and spoke to them.

The two men came back that evening.

Stefano, Nick, and Antonio had finished their shift at the docks, they waited eagerly for the two men to return. As the two men came into their room, they looked upset.

Stefano looked at them,

"What's up?"

Nicola said,

"We have smoothed things over. Let's go and tell the shopkeeper the good news."

Nick said,

"How did you manage not to pay them?"

"I just negotiated and said we would provide free food and clothing from the docks. What else could I do? These guys don't mess about. Bang, bang dead.

Barto said,

"Also, we grew up together in Sicily, my family helped them out during tough times."

They all went to see the shopkeeper and told him the news. He was so happy and the weight of the world lifted.

One day after work Antonio treated Stefano and Nick to some beers in a bar near the docks. They probably had one too many. As they left the bar laughing and swaying across the road.

They turned into Queens and from nowhere, they were being attacked. They were knocked to the ground, as these thugs attacked them.

Stefano managed to fight the person on top of him and got up and kicked the person on Nick. Nick and Antonio also fought off the men and they were all brawling in the street. Stefano recognised one of the men from the gang on the boat. Stefano made sure the man who attacked him came off worse and injured him in the fight.

The attackers had enough of a beating, they scarpered off, while the other men gave chase in their drunken states. Stefano, Nick, and Antonio had cuts, bruises, and some bloody noses. They staggered back to their room. Some of the other men were asleep and the others were working nights.

Antonio said,

"Do you think they will attack us again?

Stefano nodded,

"Revenge it's part of their culture. We must always stick together."

Nick found out from Maria that her brother was Vito Carlucci was the boss of the Black Hand Gang. This did not sit well with his values and was worried if the relationship did not turn out well, he could be killed.

Nick was struggling with the relationship and asked Maria?

"Is your brother Vito the head of the Black Hand gang?"

Maria put her arms around Nick.

"I love you, Nick, no matter what."

Nick confided in Stefano and Antonio about his future wife's family.

Stefano said,

"I love you, Nick, you are my brother. But this family kill people for fun. They create a lot of fear and violence around the city. If you don't join, you will be swimming with the fishes."

Antonio said,

"Nick, look it's up to you. But there will be no escape if they expect favours of you."

Nick finished the relationship; he was heartbroken for weeks but knew this was the right thing to do.

Stefano and the team worked on the docks with their roommates. The pay and conditions were substandard. The Italians were paid a lot less than others doing the job.

They were given the dangerous and most work for the least pay. They marched with Barto and Nicola to take their concerns to the manager about pay and conditions. The manager told them if they did not like their country, to leave and go back to their own country.

A week after three Italians died on the docks, in an accident. This highlighted the risks of working in the docks. The company did not pay one penny to the workers who died and left their families in poverty. They would not give family and workers time off, for the funeral. But all the workers downed tools, to pay their respects. The manager was furious and docked their pay. He realised that the two-union people were in big trouble. Nicola and Barto were sacked and their reputations were tarnished. Luckily the two men got jobs, through connections.

Because of poverty and hardship, some of the men in the room joined criminal gangs for survival. Poverty in those ghettos was high. Every day was survival, it was easy to understand why people turned to crime and joined mobsters.

The area was extremely dangerous and violent. People armed themselves with guns and weapons. Joining a gang meant protection and more money to feed your family.

The inequality of pay and the way people looked down on the Italians, was starting to affect the three men. Antonio still had some money and took his friends for some nice food. This helped lift their spirits. Stefano and Nick never questioned Antonio and where he got this money, they just accepted him.

One of the Italian men on the docks started complaining to the bosses about his pay, trying to feed his family. After a couple of days, the man went missing. He was never to be seen again. Rumours went around that the bosses did him in.

Journey Back 1913

Stefano needed to go back home to see his beautiful wife. After living in New York where he was treated like a rodent, a third-class citizen. Where the Italian culture was trying to be forced out on every Italian person. No wonder the Black Hand mobsters were standing up to the establishment.

Antonio was also looking forward to going back to Genoa to see his family. He never spoke of his family and no one pushed him to talk about them.

Stefano was worried for Nick. Nick wanted to stay and make a life in New York.

The Mafia wanted the life that the rich and powerful had, but as Italians were treated as low-level rats, some of the Italians took matters into their own hands. Their violence and aggression terrified the local Italian community and people paid protection money to protect their families and businesses.

Both Stefano and Antonio spent their last days in the cramped room, which they shared with another twelve men. Nick came later to spend the last night with his only family. All the men stayed up playing cards, talking, and laughing. They had some wine and pieces of cut salami.

Nick waited until he felt ready to give Stefano and Antonio a present. He had saved the money and wanted both Stefano and Nick to share thirty dollars. Both men refused, but Nick was not having it.

"I am so sad my brothers are leaving. Life is going to be hard with you both by my side."

Stefano looked at Nick,

"Nick, use these thirty dollars to come home with us."

Nick smiled,

"Everything will be okay."

It was early morning on Wednesday 5th February 1913, the men would soon have to leave to board their ship. Stefano and Antonio hugged Nick.

Antonio said,

"Thank you, Nick, for looking after me. You have been a brother to me."

Wednesday 5th February 1913- SS Canada to Naples

Both men boarded SS Canada, with their only small leather cases. All the money they had both worked for was being carried in their inner jacket lining, which was stitched by one of their friends who was a tailor. All men returning to Italy on the third class were at risk of being attacked or threatened by the Black Hand Gang. But their union friends made sure with their contacts that no one would go near them.

Before the ship set sail, both men went on deck to see New York for the last time. They waved at the Statue of Liberty and both looked at the skyline as so much building work and wooden scaffolding grew from the city. Both men had tears in their eyes. Antonio turned his head in the wild wind and rain,

"Stefano, you are doing the right thing going back home to your wife Nicolina. New York is becoming a dangerous place for us to stay. We are not liked here and are treated like rodents!

Not all Italians are mobsters, I hear they are starting a new police force and recruiting Italians to police our area of New York."

Stefano nodded,

"How about our union friends helping Italians get equal pay and helping people have rights at work? So many Italians died digging the subways, without these guys, the establishment would not care about how many people died and they did not want to spend money on safety either."

Stefano pulled his only photo of Nicolina out of his inside pocket kissed her and delicately placed his photo back in his pocket. The third class seemed less hectic than before, as fewer Italians wanted to come back. Stefano and Antonio were excited to go back home and see their families but felt bad about leaving Nick.

New York had been an exciting place, but trouble and violence were around every corner.

Stefano asked Antonio,

"You must meet my family Antonio and stay for a few days?"

"I would love to but I am homesick and can't wait to see my family in Genoa."

"Just stay two days. My family will be so pleased to meet a good man like you. You have been such a good friend. My brother Pasquale will be keen to listen to our adventures."

"Okay, Stefano, it would be an honour to meet your family. Just staying for two days."

After two weeks at sea, the men could see the port of Naples in the distance and grew excited at being home.

Meeting Stefano's Family

Both men queued in the third class as they moved through the ship and embarked into the sunshine of Naples. The noise of busy people selling their wares, and food, horse and carts driving past. Stefano glanced at the horizon and finally caught a glimpse of a familiar face; it was his brother Pasquale. He knew his wife Nicolina would be nearby. He could not hide his excitement and ran toward his brother. He ran so fast and swept Pasquale in the air, that he gave his brother a big hug. He looked around for Nicolina, then from the crowd of busy people, this sunflower shined her sunshine beam towards Stefano. He left Pasquale and moved quickly towards her; he cuddled her and held her close. They both kissed passionately and then embraced each other. Stefano held Nicolina tight, they embraced and held each other tight.

Antonio came over to Pasquale and put out his hand. Pasquale shook his hand and Antonio pulled a coin from Pasquale's ear. Pasquale smiled,

"That's magic."

Pasquale held the coin tightly in his hand like it was a precious diamond. Antonio waited for Stefano to introduce him to his wife.

"Antonio, come over here, "said Stefano.

Antonio came over took off his hat and shook Nicolina's hand.

"Pleasure to meet you, Nicolina, Stefano spoke about you all the time in New York."

"It's a pleasure to meet you, Antonio. Please come back to our house, our family would like to meet you."

Antonio flagged a horse and cart down.

"Where are we going, Pasquale said

"Grassinizi."

Nicolina said to Stefano,

"These carriages are expensive."

Antonio chipped in,

"It's no problem I will pay, my treat."

Pasquale sat next to Antonio and asked him all about America. He was so excited about the magic trick, that he asked Antonio to keep doing it.

Stefano and Nicolina took in all the sites and scenery. Stefano could smell home. He sat holding Nicolina's hand until they arrived at Grazzinizzi. As soon as he could see his parent's home, he bet Pasquale could not beat him in a race to their home. Pasquale and Stefano jumped off the carriage and raced to their home.

Pasquale just won, and then Stefano's parents came out and hugged Stefano. Nicolina's parents came over and hugged Stefano.

Then the carriage stopped outside their homes, Antonio paid the man and came over to meet everybody. He shook hands with Stefano's parents and kissed them on both cheeks, which was customary in Naples.

Stefano said,

"This is one of my best friends alongside Nick and I said he could stay here for a few days."

Pasquale pulled on Antonio's arm and started asking him lots of questions about America.

Stefano's family made Antonio welcome in their small apartment. Stefano and Nicolina would both sleep at her parent's apartment, to make space for Antonio sleeping over.

Antonio took Pasquale to the local bakery and butcher to buy some food. He got Pasquale and himself a coffee and a cake before returning home.

All the women prepared the table outside. That evening Stefano's parents cooked a beautiful meal with pasta and steak, and they drank their homemade wine. They sat on long benches put together. The men sat down and poured the homemade wine out of the demijohns. The women prepared the food in the tiniest of spaces and served the men a bigger portion of food, than their plates.

Everyone made Antonio feel comfortable. Everybody just relaxed in the beautiful sunshine.

Stefano looked around the table at his family, he had missed them so much.

"This was heaven, all the important people in my life, around this table. I miss Nick and wish he could be here. There was something different from the Grazzinissi sunshine to the New York sunshine. Our sun is warm, and kind and gives you love and kisses. It's so good to be back with my beautiful wife and family."

Paolo lifts his wine glass,

"Salute, my family."

They all ate, drank, and laughed. Stefano and Antonio told them of their adventures in New York. Stefano held Nicolina's hand and did not want to let her go, as he had missed her so much.

After each course, all the women would bring the next dish. They eat and drink into the night. Nicolina's dad started the singing off with Neapolitan folk and love songs.

They all stayed up till three in the morning. Antonio fell asleep at the table. In the morning, he woke up to empty tables. He woke up at six, to find no one around. He got up and walked through the village, one lady said that Stefano and his family were working on the land. The lady took Antonio to the land and he thanked the woman.

Stefano came over,

"Morning friend. Hope you slept okay."

"That wine helped. Can I help you on the land?"

"Yeah, sure."

They all worked in the burning sunshine till lunchtime. It was too hot to work and they all returned home for a siesta.

On the way home Antonio said,

"Yesterday was such an amazing day, I will never forget it. The people, food, and conversation. You have a lovely family."

Stefano smiled,

"They are everything to me, they are my faith. You are part of my family Antonio; you have been a good friend to me."

You have been a good friend to me also. But tonight, I will have to leave for Genoa."

"I will miss you, Antonio."

That evening Antonio said his goodbyes and kissed everyone. A local farmer offered to take him to Naples on his horse and cart.

He climbed up and waved goodbye, he looked back at Stefano and Nicolina. Pasquale had also climbed onto the horse cart and decided to ride with them to Naples.

Antonio liked Pasquale, he was such a great kid, and he never stopped asking questions.

World War 1 (1914-18).

In May 1915, Italy entered World War I and attacked Austria-Hungary along the Isonzo River. Luigi Cadorna (Chief of Staff of the Italian Army) gave the orders for the attack. Stefano completed his eight weeks of basic training and was assigned to the Alpini specialist unit for further mountaineer training.

Nick had come back from New York and enlisted in the Army. He joined Stefano two months later. Two months after Nick, Antonio joined his pals in the freezing mountainous terrain. They were all assigned to the Alpini specialist unit for further mountaineering training, then posted along the Isonzo River, across the vast landscape of treacherous snow and ice mountains. As part of the Alpini unit, they were issued with extra winter clothing, climbing ropes, and skiing equipment.

Over the next months, artillery guns and weapons had to be pulled up the steep mountain peaks, in freezing conditions. It seemed an impossible place to fight a war or win a battle. Fast-flowing rivers from glaciers and minimal road and train connection to the area. The Alpini and Italian army worked laboriously to build the paths, roads, and rail networks. As well as build huts, forts, and barracks for the men. Stefano and his pals used explosives to create networks of caves, for protection, accommodation, and storage.

Cable cars were set up and mules were to transport food, and munitions and to help the wounded down where army hospitals were. It was now October and temperatures remained below freezing. Along with winter came the dark nights, in which artillery and explosions lit up the skies. The Alpini specialist ski units equipped their soldiers with ice picks, ropes, snowsuits, cold-weather clothing, and goggles to support their patrols on the glaciers.

As winter came, the extreme conditions caused cold injuries, frostbite, and hypothermia which were a real problem for all men in the high Alps, especially when it came to treating the wounded, who suffered terribly from the extreme conditions. Combat was very difficult under these circumstances. Artillery could not accurately identify enemy targets due to the uneven terrain, and without effective artillery fire, it was extremely difficult to launch a successful attack. The fighting was fierce, in which Stefano and his pals were involved in hand-to-hand fighting and gas attacks.

The mountain peaks and glacial ice needed great skill. On Friday 13th December 1916, Stefano and his team heard a rumbling in the mountains, they hid in a tunnel dug by the engineers. Then they heard the noise of tons of snow and ice falling down the mountain like ice cream flowing down a cone. There were screams and shouting as the avalanche killed men all down the mountain.

1917

In September 1917, Pasquale had been posted also to the Alpini regiment. Stefano was unaware that his brother was enlisting.

Stefano, Nick and Antonio, and their unit had just returned from a ferocious bloody battle, all the men returned silently at the horrors they had just witnessed. As Stefano entered the barrack room now as a sergeant, he saw his brother Pasquale. Stefano went to his brother and hugged him and would not let go of him.

"What you doing here Pasquale, I don't want you here in this terrible war."

Pasquale looked so innocent.

"I am here for the same reason you are, to serve my country."

"I cannot believe you are here in this hell hole and freezing temperatures."

He hugged his younger brother and introduced him to all the men. Over the month, Pasquale soon becomes one of the men. He soon was part of the skirmishes.

In October 1917 the Alpini unit was sent to Caporetto, sixty miles north of Trieste. There was a fixed machine gun on the Austrian-Hungary mountain peak. The guns looked down this sheer peak, with limited cover and extreme conditions the Alpini unit moved slowly on their enemy. The machine guns just wiped out the men below. Just as Stefano went to move to Pasquale's cover point. Machine gun fire ripped into the men ascending the sheer rocky edge of the mountain.

The machine gun bullets haled down on the Italian troops, men dying and taking their last breath. Then Stefano heard a scream, it was a familiar sound.

He moved across the steep edge of this mountain, checking on his men. When he saw Pasquale lying down with blood all around him.

"Pasquale," Stefano shouted.

"Medic."

Antonio and Nick made their way to Stefano, who was hugging Pasquale and crying. The Medic did his best, but Pasquale passed away in the freezing snow. All the men helped lower Pasquale's body down the glacier and tried their best to console Stefano. The machine gun continued to kill thousands from the peak. Stefano decided enough was enough, he was going to get revenge for killing his brother. He put grenades and explosives in a rucksack. He told Antonio and Nick to stay put, he did not want them to help him on this mission.

“This is something I must do alone. I don’t want any more people to die.”

Nick held Stefano back,

“We are all in this together, Pasquale was my brother also.”

Stefano, Nick, and Antonio carried a sack of explosives and made the climb up the mountain until they were just under the machine guns. The freezing conditions did not stop these men who were now in a dangerous position. The machine guns roared and sent fire like from a dragon's mouth on the men below.

Stefano, Nick, and Antonio prepped and set the explosives and then they all threw the explosives into the dugouts where the machine guns were situated. After throwing the explosives, they all made a quick descent under an overhanging ledge.

The explosions all detonated and sent debris of rocks, human flesh, and blood down the mountain. The machine guns were silent and an eerie silence of death and despair filled the void. Blood stained the pure white snow, over the mountain. Stefano, Nick, and Antonio had saved all their men below.

Stefano and his pals made their way back down the mountain to help rescue his men, with hand-to-hand fighting. He helped all his unit escape as they made their way into a tunnel.

After the war, Stefano was awarded the Purple Heart for bravery. Nick went back to New York and Antonio went back to Genoa.

Stefano went home with the sad loss of his brother Pasquale. He felt such guilt and was ashamed that he had to tell his parents that they had lost a son. He went home to his beautiful wife Nicolina.

Old Curiosity Shop- Old Kent Road

Sitting in a tailor's booth, with the dull brown curtain pulled across the rail. Antonio sat breathing heavily, sweating and in shock at what he had just witnessed. He held his Alpini cap tightly in his left hand and just started to cry.

Two well-dressed men in black suits, black ties and cufflinks stood outside the curtain, with tape measures draping around both their necks. One of the tailors was thin with grey hair and a moustache and the other was rotund with dark hair and a beard. They gently pulled the curtain back and the thin tailor comforted Antonio, while the other poured Antonio a cup of tea. He patted Antonio on his shoulder.

"Time travelling back in time, is an amazing emotional journey of pain and sorrow as this is your flesh and blood. This experience will change you, as you have seen what a brave adventurous Nonno he was. He stood by his values."

Antonio rubbed his eyes,

"I should have saved Pasquale. My Granddad saved all his men by attacking the machine guns, that were fixed on top of the mountain. He was so generous, and kind and loved his family. I cannot believe where I have been. I feel so humble and proud of my Nonno and my Nonna, so much love for these amazing family members."

The rotund tailor smiled,

"Your Nonno is so proud of you, in all the adversity of your Nonno, you were there. He is so proud of you and he wanted you to have this."

He handed him a small leather case.

Antonio opened the leather case to find a medal, a purple heart medal.

"The Purple Heart medal was only given to Italian soldiers in World War I, for extreme bravery. This was only given to a few."

The tailors bought Antonio's clothes in and placed them on the clothes hook fastened on the wall.

Both tailors patted Antonio on his shoulders. The rotund tailor bent down and spoke

"Your Nonno was a brave, kind family man."

Both tailors left the cubicle and pulled the curtain too. Antonio gently hung the clothes the tailors had given him to time travel in. He put on his jeans and T-shirt and his sports trainers. His phone and money were inside his jeans pocket. He picked up the leather case, looked inside and studied the medal, engraved was his Nonno's name, Stefano Russo.

He pulled back the curtains and the two tailors smiled and opened the front door for Antonio.

He stepped out of the Old Curiosity Shop on the Old Kent Road, in the hustle and bustle of this busy road. He looked towards the tailor shop, which had now changed to an antique shop.

Funky Angel

It is one of those cold wintry nights, the type of cold air where you can see your breath. Yet most of the locals who went into the Park Tavern pub was wearing t-shirts. The pub was heaving with young and old, every type of character. Football fans who were drunk, chanting sadistic songs patriotic to their cause. Gangsters who marked their turf and put fear into anybody who wanted to get in their way. Fear meant respect and keeping a hand on the deals in the streets. Do you know what happens if you get out of line?

These Gangsters marking their turf are modern; fashionable and love to flash the cash and drugs. They knew how to intimidate people and most locals kept their distance from them.

Unfortunately, on this night there are two rival gang leaders in the same heaving pub, John Angel, and Psycho Whitfield.

They both clocked each other across the bar. Their eyes set on battle, mortal combat, adrenalin rushing and the atmosphere was tense. John moves away from the girl he is talking to. She is Psycho's ex-girlfriend. Psycho likes to control people and girlfriends; she belongs to him only and he wants revenge. No one gets his possessions.

Psycho eyeballs John and goes over to him. They square up to each other, for a battle. The tension around them is heavy, both with glaring eyes and flaring nostrils like gladiators in an arena. Locals move out of their space, fearful of any backlash. The violent volcano erupts as the two men explode into violence. Punches are thrown with a velocity, trying to inflict pain on each other.

The fight spills out of the pub into the cold winter air. One man grabs a bottle from an outside table and Johns's crew disarms him.

They both end up on the ground grappling and punching each other. The crowd of on-lookers spill from the pub and gather around this violent brawl.

The crowd watches excitedly; as though they are watching a violent movie on their large high-definition screens.

Kiely Angel is John's brother, an aspiring DJ by night and a plumber by day. It's Saturday evening and he is making his way to the Park Tavern pub, to meet John and have a drink with him. He is going to have a drink with his brother before going to work as a DJ at the Hero Caine club. As Kiely approaches the pub, he witnesses the violent brawl of fists.

He feels sick in the pit of his stomach; as he recognises one of the men. It is his brother John. He was fighting a lad they call Psycho; a notorious gang leader, with a love for violence. Kiely was scared, his body felt heavy like his legs were made of lead. In an angry rage, he runs into the battlefield arena. He starts to fight Psycho.

John continues to throw a combination of punches and kicks. The on-looking crowd was getting their fill of entertainment. Both men now have blood on their shirts. Police sirens can now be heard and the fighters stop. Psycho stands tall and defiant. He makes his hand into the shape of a gun, and he gestures and points his hand to John. He smiles and pretends to pull the trigger.

He shouts,

"Dead, dead, you're dead.

Psycho runs off as he does not want the police involved.

John walks to Psycho's ex, who is crying from watching the violence. He comforts her.

"It's okay babe; he won't bother you again."

The onlookers try to show John that they are on his side.

One person mumbles,

"If you need any help with Psycho; I'm on your side."

John just nods. He fully understands that no one will help you; it is all talk. With blood on his dark shirt; John embraces his brother Kiely.

"I know fighting is not your scene, but you saved my bacon bruv. Mum and Dad always said you were an Angel by name and by nature."

Kiely was still feeling anxious with fear and full of adrenaline. He looked directly at his brother.

"Family is everything, but I can't do this all the time. I am worried about your life; you are too precious and smart for all this gang stuff."

The police did not stop at the Park Tavern. John continued as if nothing had happened and pulled Julia and Kiely back into the pub.

The pub manager did not say a word; he was scared that he may be targeted by violence from either gang.

Park Tavern

Back inside the Park Tavern, life goes back to normal. Football fans are singing in the corner and John is at the bar chatting with Julia. Kiely goes over to John and says hi to some of the locals.

"Bruv, what was that fight all about?"

John smiled,

"This is Julia; she's the love of my life."

Kiely recognized Julia,

"Didn't you go out with Psycho Whitfield?"

Julia hesitantly replied,

"Yeah, but I must have been mad because he is off his rocker and violently scary. I never want to see him again."

Kiely pulls John to one side,

"Are you crazy bruv? Do you know who her ex is?

"Kiely listen, her ex is history. I'm not scared of him. Now chill, I am going to buy some gear."

Kiely hated the thought of John doing drugs,

"You don't need that stuff to have a good time."

John laughed,

"I need it for that garage music you play."

John nodded to a well-known dealer and went to the toilets. Kiely continued chatting with Julia. Psycho makes a re-appearance in the pub. Everybody stops talking; silence fills the pub with fear. Julia looks in horror, knowing what violence he is capable of. Psycho is stocky with cropped hair, baggy jeans, a stylish top and trainers.

Psycho has a scar above his eyebrow and scars over his head. He notices Julia straight away and walks towards her and Kiely. He eyeballed Kiely and then wedged himself between them. He turned to Julia,

"You've been avoiding me, sweetness."

Julia looked away nervously.

"I'm not your possession any more, and we are finished for good."

She began to shake with fear and started to cry uncontrollably.

Psycho tipped her drink over her head.

"No one finishes with me, got it bitch."

Kiely interrupted,

"Didn't you hear her, you are finished."

Psycho grabbed Kiely by his throat. John now out of the toilet sees Psycho and runs over and continues the fight. He throws punches into Psycho's head.

The fight explodes in this limited space. Psycho seemed to be enjoying himself and revelling in this violence; like a warrior in battle. Psycho then just stopped fighting and once again turned to John and made a sign of a gun with his hand

and pretended to pull the trigger. Psycho left the pub. Kiely grabbed John and Julia,

"Let's get out of here quick, through the back way."

They flagged down a taxi, as snow started to fall into the cold air.

"John, I am worried. What have we got involved in? Let's get to my club?"

John is jubilant with his battle and oblivious to Kiely's fear and worry.

"I would have had him you know."

John put his arm around Julia and looked into her eyes,

"I will never let him do that again, love you babe."

Julia wiped away her tears "love you too"

Kiely told the taxi driver,

"To the Hero Caine Club, please mate."

The taxi driver nodded. Kiely remained silent with fear and tried to take in what had just happened.

Hero Caine Club

The taxi drops them outside the Hero Caine Club, and Kiely pays the driver. They walk past the queue of people waiting to get into the club. Kiely walks to the front door and gives a big high-five to all the lads at the door. His boss Antonio was also there. Antonio was from a well-known gangland family; but was fond of Kiely.

He notices that John has been in a fight. He knows that Kiely is a good kid and decides not to ask John the question.

"What's happening Kiely, hopefully, you are going to play some good music for a change."

He laughs and so does all the lads on the door.

"Only joshing Kiely; you know you are the best."

Kiely introduced John and his girlfriend Julia. Antonio turned to John,

"You are lucky to have a brother like Kiely; you must listen to him; he talks a lot of sense. Now jog on guys, work to do"

"Thanks, Guv, laters yeah."

Kiely led John and Julia to the bar. Kiely is not on till midnight and went to the bar with John to get a drink.

He turned to John,

"How about getting a real job, working as my apprentice? Plumbing is a trade for life and will give you a good wage."

"I know I need to get my act together. Of course, I will be your apprentice. Now get us a drink as I am going for a wazz."

"Don't be taking any of that stuff up your nose,"

John ignored him. The club was now getting busy. Sweaty bodies dancing, vibrant lights. music is pumping and bouncing off all the walls.

Kiely was popular at the club and knew a lot of the regulars. He stops to chat with a woman that he grew up with called Celia. They swap numbers. Kiely has always had a soft spot for Celia and planned to call her later to arrange a date.

Psycho & Friends

Kiely left John and Julia, to get ready to prepare for his shift on the decks. John was out of his head and all over Julia. He grabs Julia.

Julia is very drunk "what's up honey."

"Julia listens, Psycho's turned up with his mob. Get Kiely quick."

Psycho spotted John and Julia and his pals moved towards them.

Psycho laughed.

"Hello John, you are in big trouble son. On your way Julia, silly little bitch, stupid bitch, dead bitch."

Julia grabbed John,

"I'm not going anywhere."

Psycho frowned,

"It's okay Julia, we don't discriminate against who we do-over. You know I am going to do lover boy good and proper."

Kiely spotted Psycho and his mob and signalled for the bouncers. Psycho is soon surrounded by a mob of bouncers, which did not faze Psycho. He and his mob are asked to leave.

Psycho laughed and he gave the nod to his pals, who followed him to the main entrance.

The bouncers followed and escorted them out of the club. Kiely went with the bouncers to make sure. This made him feel anxious and worried for John's life.

Psycho and his mob are nasty people. As Psycho left the club, he briefly turned around to face the main door entrance.

He looked at Kiely and once again made a sign of a gun with his fingers and pulled the trigger and laughed. This left an eerie cold chill over Kiely.

He knows this guy won't stop until he gets revenge. He needs to get back to his decks; this is his creative escape from the outside world. Kiely gives a brilliant DJ session and rocked the house with his music and humour.

John and Julia decided at two am to get a taxi home.

Kiely worked till three and sent a text,

"Don't forget you will be starting your apprenticeship on Monday and be careful John."

Work Finished

Kiely finished his shift and was buzzing after his stunning performance. Kiely walks to the main entrance saying his goodbyes to everyone. The boss Antonio was at the main entrance.

"That was fantastico Kiely. There was some trouble earlier, everything ok?"

"Well, this gang whose leader Psycho is after my brother John; Psycho is a real nut job. John needs to have to watch himself."

Antonio lit a cigarette and commented,

"You will need to watch yourself and be careful. You are a smart kid; don't get involved with all that rubbish."

"I will be on my guard Antonio, honest. I'm ready to go home for a kip."

"You want me to get you a taxi?"

"It's okay boss; I'm going to walk home to clear my head. Listen boss appreciate the concern, I'll be okay."

Kiely made his way out of the club past the drunken stragglers for the journey home. He decided to send a text to Celia,

"Will call you tomorrow. I have always been your number one fan xx."

Kiely heard the tyres of a car screech behind him and someone calling his name. There was a blanket of snow; he could see his breath in the air. He stopped and tried to make out the face in the car. A message buzzed on his phone.

Then several gunshots exploded and the now cool air turned completely black and the snow was stained red.

St Peter's Gate

Kiely opened his eyes, he blinked several times, confused about what had just happened and where he was?

He was at the reception centre, where an old-fashioned nurse was checking him over.

Then this bloke appears dressed in a two-tone suit and a Mod Parka, wearing Hush Puppies shoes. He looked like Paul Weller.

The Mod introduced himself;

"Hello Kiely, I am St. Peter."

Kiely thought I must have had too much to drink or I was losing the plot. He could smell the garlic.

St. Peter reassured Kiely with empathy and put his arm around him.

"This will be a big shock to you, but you were shot by Psycho and his gang.

I am sorry to tell you that the paramedics could not save you and you rose to our Heaven Reception Centre."

Kiely looked for a door to get back to his home, but it was no use.

Kiely angrily shouted,

"St. Peter would never be a Mod, where're your wings? Now let me go!"

St Peter laughed,

"I do have wings but all angels can conceal them well."

Kiely witnessed the magnificent wings as they appeared from St. Peter. A brilliant light glistened on his wings. He flew across the room with ease and put a DVD in the player.

"Soon I will show you a DVD of your life from childhood to the present.

I am very proud to have a great person join us in Heaven."

"You have footage of me, even as a child?"

St. Peter smiled,

"We can even go back to when you were in your mother's tummy. I also have a special favour to ask after the Heaven induction program. I believe you have the right attributes to join the Angel Defense Force. The Angel Defense Force is a new service developed by our glorious boss because things on Earth are getting out of hand. We need special Angels to be placed back on Earth to address these problems. How about it, Kiely? You don't have to make your mind up just yet."

Kiely still in shock replied,

"You're saying I have died and in Heaven and you want me to join the Angel Defense Force. Heaven has an induction course; where am I, am I in a hospital in a coma?"

St. Peter reassured Kiely,

"The induction course is there to ensure your eternal life in Heaven."

"So, if I am in Heaven, can I play football with Pele, George Best and Bobby Moore?"

St. Peter smiled,

"All in good time. However, if you do accept to join the Angel Defense Force, you will be put through your paces to attain your specialized wings.

You will be put through a lot of real-life situations that will be unusual and varied. If you pass all these tests, you will be awarded your Angel Defense Wings."

"I will do anything to get back to Earth and see my family and brother."

St. Peter gave the thumbs up to Kiely,

"I am very proud that you want to join the Angel Defense Force, but it will be an emotional journey. You will soon understand that time is not the same in Heaven; you can time travel back and forth through time.

If you are successful in completing the Angel Defense Force test; you will find yourself with a nice set of wings and I can assign you to other important missions and a few pints in Heaven's Mod bar."

Kiely laughed,

"Who would have thought that St. Peter likes a pint."

St. Peter looked at his watch,

"After the induction course, there will be no time to waste and you will be ready for your first mission."

Induction Course

Kiely could not believe he was sitting in a comfortable lounge watching a DVD of his whole life. Tears streamed down his face as he looked at his wonderful family. He watched the DVD up to being shot and realised the text message must have come from Celia.

The DVD showed his brother John; who had got mixed up with the wrong dangerous people. Kiely was angry, because of this gang warfare he was now dead. John was now in danger of his life.

St. Peter came in and comforted Kiely,

"There is something you can do to help. We need someone special like you to join this new team. It is simply good against bad; your role will help reduce problems such as drugs, crime, poverty, and disease. To be part of this wonderful team you must complete all the missions we set you; no matter how crazy they may seem."

Kiely rubbed his eyes,

"Am I dreaming? You have an elite team of Angels and I must pass some sort of SAS test to get in."

St. Peter fixed his collar of his Ben Sherman shirt,

"Not quite SAS or military training. These are tests or scenarios that you will encounter; covering all walks of life, society, and people. I am here to guide you and be your coach. There are too many bad things happening on Earth. We need good people like you to make a difference. I am here to help you become an Angel."

"You don't want much. If I say yes, will I really play football with the greats? You know Pele, Johan Cruyff, Peter Osgood, and George Best?"

St. Peter laughed,

" No problem, once you've passed the test; you will be given your angel wings and I will arrange for you to play football with the greats. Could you sign this contract?"

"No problem guv, at least it gets me back to Earth."

St. Peter gave Kiely a high five;

"The final stage will be difficult, painful but that is all I can tell you.

If you come into this room Kiely, you will be prepared for your first mission shortly.

St. Peter looked at his watch,

"Blimey, I'm late. Sorry Kiely, no time to explain. You need to go straight into your first mission. Godspeed and I will be there at times to support you."

First Mission

Transported back to familiar territory, Kiely was in his hometown. It is the same hometown, with lots of traffic, smells of exhausts, red buses pulling out into the busy traffic and the hustle and bustle of people. Kiely is just standing and staring in amazement. His lungs take big gulps of air, in which he expels the air with great pleasure. Feeling elated, but also extremely emotional about the prospect of coming back as a visitor. Looking down this familiar street; the chatter in his head was saying,

"It's hard to believe the journey so far. One minute I'm here and then I get killed and now back here as a potential angel."

He runs down this road and shouts,

"I'm alive."

People who were passing, looked awkwardly at Kiely making sure they skirted around this person. He was running down the familiar road, which takes you to the Hero Caine Club.

St. Peter gave Kiely a heaven credit card to get money out and be authentic in his new role. Stopping outside a bank, he withdrew two hundred pounds out. He then saw the Hero Caine Club sign. He cautiously goes to the front of the building and starts to feel tears streaming down his face. He notices a poster on the windows, DJ wanted. Kiely rings the intercom and notices the club sign was under new management, all enquiries to go through to Harry Snatch. Harry was a violent psycho, who loved drugs and violence. Harry answers the intercom,

"Yeah."

"I have seen the poster in the window for the DJ job."

"OK, come up to my office."

"Where is your office"?

No answer, the buzzer to the door rings and Kiely enters the darkly lit club.

There is an office with Guvnor on it; Kiely knocks on the door.

"Come in."

Kiely enters a dimly lit room. He can see a silhouette of a figure. Harry has his back to him, looking out of the window and rocking side to side on his leather office chair. This person is stocky in build and Kiely senses the man's tension.

"I have come for the DJ job."

"Is that right; any good?"

"Really good."

The Guvnor points to a set of decks in the corner of his dark-lit office.

"Show me what you can do."

Kiely goes to the decks and strokes the decks with pride. He switches everything on and funks the room out with the records near the decks.

"What's your DJ name then"?

"I am called Funky Angel."

Harry laughs out loud,

"Funky Angel. You know I run a tight ship here and problems could mean my crew will be your worst nightmare."

"Your business is your business. I'm just going to be concentrating on putting the F into Funky."

Harry lights up a cigar and quickly grabs Kiely by the throat.

"You will be good for the club, but mess me around and I will eat you alive."

"I know the score boss."

"Welcome aboard Mr Funky Angel Man, do you want one of my cakes."

"No thanks, I'm on a diet"

Harry laughs out aloud;

"Nice to see someone who says no to me. You have got balls, son. You start tonight; £200 a night and free gear?"

Kiely takes the job and leaves the club. Kiely was just so amazed at how wonderful it was to be back in his home town.

Kiely surprisingly sees a group of people he knows. He approaches them;

“Guys, how’s things?”

He waits excitedly for a familiar response.

They all stared at him like he was a stranger.

“Rob, it’s me Kiely Angel”

“Get away from me, before I knock your lights out. Kiely’s dead. My mate was dead all right!”

“I am sorry, sorry mate.” No one recognises me, I don’t bloody exist, and I don’t exist.”

Tears flooded down Kiely’s face. Passersby moved away from him, by looking anywhere except in the direction of Kiely.

“I’m not mad, I am an angel. I am here to help you.”

A passerby points to his head,

"You're off your rocker son."

Kiely boards the tube at Southfields and recognises a girl that he thought has passed away.

"Suzy it's me Kiely."

"Hiya Kiely; lovely to see you again."

"I thought you had passed away. Didn't you have a drug overdose?"

"I'm fine now; clean as a whistle" and laughs.

"You can see me, can't you?"

"Course I can Kiely."

She got off the next station. Kiely looks in amazement. Suzy blows him a kiss.

Kiely goes into the Park Tavern pub, for a pint,

"Pint please mate."

Kiely looks over and sees Julia with some friends; he goes over, to see if he can find out about John.

“Is your name Julia?”

“Yes.”

“Do you know someone called John Angel?”

Julia bursts into tears.

“What’s up Julia, I didn’t mean anything by it.”

The pub goes silent. The barman comes around the bar and grabs Kiely;

“Get out of my pub and stay out.”

Kiely is left feeling lonely and sad. This place does not seem familiar anymore and flags down a taxi to go to the Hero Caine club.

Hero Caine Club

Kiely arrives at the Hero Caine Club and goes straight to Harry Snatch's Office. Harry was sitting in very poor lighting and smoking a cigar.

"I'm glad you have come early; the last DJ is swimming with the fishes. That's what happens to those who think they are clever. He was a grass and couldn't be trusted. Now get yourself a drink and you start in ten minutes."

"I won't let you down Guv; honest."

"I know you won't; especially when your life is on the line."

He snorts a line of white powder then looks to the ceiling and laughs uncontrollably.

Kiely makes his way to the stage and checks the DJ equipment and checks the microphone.

"How are you guys and dolls doing? The Funky Angel is here to bless you with my sounds."

Kiely puts the music on and then sees John walking past the stage. He looks in amazement and steps down from the platform,

"John it's me Kiely!"

John shrugs past Kiely's.

"My brother is dead, if I hear you pretend to be my brother, I will punch your lights out."

"John it's me your brother."

"I have just lost my brother and I advise you to move away now before I get violent. Now, jog on arsehole!"

Kiely went back to his decks and played John's favourite garage remix record. John froze in silence and felt a cold shiver through his body. He went towards Kiely.

"How do you know this is my favourite remix; who are you."

"I'm a close friend of your brothers."

"I've not seen you before."

"He asked me to keep an eye on you."

"Listen, mate, I can look after myself."

"I know you can, but if you need any help or you want to talk; I'm here for you."

"I've got some business to sort out all right. Laters mate. What's your name?"

"Eh, call me Jules."

John straightens his jacket; Kiely notices he has a gun in a holster tucked under his right arm.

"Are you carrying a gun?"

"Keep it down, will you? You need protection in this business."

"Having a gun will only attract trouble. Do you want to die or do a stretch in prison?

"You sound like my brother; laters geezer."

Kiely goes back to his decks and notices that John is heading for Harry's office.

Harry prepares some Bolivian Charlie and gestures it to John. Harry laughs for no reason and divvies up a few lines for snorting. They both begin to snort the cocaine through rolled-up twenty-pound notes.

"That's some stuff, Harry."

"You what?"

"Heavy shit man. Well, I've got plenty of that heavy shit. I want you to be my right-hand man. I need you to be out there selling."

"No thanks, Harry; I'm my own man. No hard feelings; things are ok as they are."

John looks around and then Harry pulls out a gun and points it at John. Harry pulls the trigger and a flame comes out.

"You tosser Harry. I thought you were going to shoot me dead."

Harry laughs and hands John a parcel. John takes the parcel and walks through the club.

Kiely sees John leave Harry's office with this parcel and realises that his brother John was selling drugs for Harry.

Then there is a familiar smell of garlic and St. Peter appeared dancing next to him.

"My life is in danger St. Peter; what do I do next and how do I protect my brother?"

"Kiely, you are a brave young man and you are showing great bravery. This is the hardest test of all because it involves family. You are trying to help and make this place a better one, by firstly steering your family members away from trouble. With your good positive outlook and great people skills, there is always a chance of improving people's misfortune."

"St. Peter do you believe I can help and give hope; especially to those who lead a life of drugs and violence."

"I strongly believe you have what it takes, to communicate to people of all levels. I know you felt let down when your Dad passed away from cancer; because the hope that you had was taken away from you. But miracles can happen."

"I put all my hope and prayers into my Dad not dying. If my Dad was alive now, John would not be mixing with this lot."

"I know I can't bring your Dad to life. I know he loves you and John very much. One day you will meet your Dad, I promise."

"I would give anything to see my Dad again. My Dad used to take me and John everywhere. He made everything fun and safe. Mum found it so difficult after Dad died."

"I am so sorry Kiely; losing a parent when you were so young was a big trauma in your life. You will get the chance to meet your Dad at some point. I will arrange it with the main man, honestly. Now listen you need to concentrate on the music. I think Harry is coming over."

"If you are telling the truth about seeing my Dad; then I am ready to take anything on board."

"You have my word. Bless you, my son. Is there any chance of you playing Happy Jack by the Who?"

"You have three hopes; Bob Hope, envelope, and no hope. There is no way I am jeopardising my career even when I don't exist."

Harry Snatch summons Kiely to his office. He blows cigar smoke into Kiely's face. "I've got a proposition for you. I like a kid who has balls like you; Mr. Funky Angel. I need someone like you to drive my other business; I know you would be good."

"Do you mean running drugs?"

"Watch your mouth or else. I can make you a rich man. You see the guy I've got now, has been doing me out of pocket, no what I mean? That loser will be swimming with the fishes soon."

"Do you mean John was going to be swimming with the fishes?"

"He has been undercutting my business; he wants a big stash of the pie. John's a real fox. Don't you worry his cards are marked? I need someone that I can trust; like you Mr. Funky Angel man."

"I can't win here whatever I do; violence will be the outcome of all this."

Harry leans over his desk and blows more cigar smoke at Kiely.

"I am offering you the chance to become a rich man. All the riches you want plus freebies. What more do you want?"

"I will need to sleep on it first Guv; before I can give you an answer."

Kiely needed more time to think about what to do. Harry pulls out a wad of cash and puts the lot in front of Kiely.

"This is yours; consider it a gift. All you have to do is deliver some packages; that's it. Leave John to me; I want the satisfaction of finishing him off."

"You can keep your money; I want no part in your world. John seems like a nice kid who has just got in with the wrong crowd."

Harry pulls out a gun;

"You have no choice Funky Angel; you are in it up to your nuts. Everything has your prints on. You are in for one long jail sentence."

"You don't scare me mate. I am just here for the music."

"Watch your back son; as you never know who might put a knife in it."

He snorts some more lines of cocaine and collapses on his desk. Kiely goes back to his decks.

John returns agitated and angry. He goes over to Kiely at the decks;

"Yeah man, all right and that. I've just made some money Mr DJ."

"What do you mean you have made some money?"

"I have made some notes today. I'm on top of the world and no one is going to take me down."

"You seem a bit out of it and uptight."

"What you talking about?

"Look if you ever need to talk about anything; I am here for you."

"I want to talk man; Barrack Obama guy was a genius. He is the type of guy who uses his brain; he wouldn't get in a barney straight away. He would talk his way out of it.

You see in this business; death is part of the employment contract."

"Who wants you dead John?"

"Scratch and Sniff wants me brown bread. He thinks I have got too big for my boots. But the truth is that he knows I can take him and the business."

"John, it is not worth risking your life, is it? You have got to get away from here."

"I don't run from anyone; you with me or what?"

"I will always help you, John; but violence is not the answer."

"That's what my brother would have said."

"It seems like your brother talked a lot of sense."

"Sometimes you've got to make a stand from bullies like Snatch. There is no other word to describe these cockroaches of society. He kills people, straight up. By drugs or by a gun, he's ruthless and will blow your brains out, without a care in the world.

Because of this violent and ruthless person, he is respected by the threatened community.

It's time to do some good. I am going to save all those young people from violence, drugs, and alcohol. Yeah, I am making a stand of good against filth and scum."

"Things can change John; you can change your life and do the right thing. I am behind you."

"Do you think I can change and do good things?"

"I believe you can be better than that Harry scum bag. You are a smart lad."

John grabs one of the microphones;

"Snatch you dirty stinking rat. I am on top of the world and nobody is going to take me down. This empire belongs to me now; if you want to keep it you will have to fight me, man. Yeah, come and try to take me down."

Harry Snatch hears John shouting his head off. He loads his gun and goes downstairs and places himself between Kiely and John.

"What game are you playing? I think you've played the death card. Yeah, you don't value your life, do you?"

John pulls his gun;

"Stand back; don't make me blow your brains all over the dance floor."

Kiely moves in front of John.

"John, calm down man; don't do anything stupid."

There is a mass panic on the dance floor, as the audience head for the exits.

"You were nothing when you came here. Go on pull the trigger; I have got nothing to live for. Go on, pull the trigger."

John moves closer to Harry;

"Don't tempt me. One shot to take a filthy killing scum bag off the streets."

"You think you're a saint; when you have just sold a load of gear off tonight. Who have you sold drugs to?

I will tell you; tonight, Matthew young people will be shooting up in their arms; so that you can have loads of money and to think that you are someone special."

"John, I beg you don't do it."

Kiely stands in front of John. Harry sees an opening and grabs John. They both wrestle each other to the ground. Kiely tries to intervene and then a gunshot is fired.

John, John, John speaks to me, man. There is no answer from John, he has blood pooling around him. Kiely falls to his knees and cradles his brother closely.

"John it's me your brother; I love you man; now wake up. My beautiful brother; I have let you down."

St. Peter appeared and turned the lights on.

"Kiely please relax; everything is not what it seems. Everyone here has put on an Oscar performance."

"What's going on; are you saying…?"

John gets up from the floor. Kiely, I'm fine honest. I am so pleased this is over; we are all so proud of you. I love you man and am so pleased to see you again."

St. Peter moves towards the brothers,

"Let me explain. Kiely, everything in this Hero Caine club has been acted out. You see as part of the Angel Defense Force I wanted to test you to see if you could lead this special unit. Dealing with family was the hardest thing to deal with and you have passed with flying colours. You are a natural leader.

"I thought the Angel Defense Force was for people who have passed away?"

"Kiely, I am so sorry that this news could not be disclosed earlier. But everyone in this club has died from some sort of violent crime, drugs, or alcohol incident. I will let John explain..."

"That night I left your club with Psycho's ex; a car pulled up beside me and shot me three times.

It was Psycho and his gang. I died there and then. You were right bruv; all this gang stuff is a load of bullshit. Now that I have made it to Heaven; I have learnt the error of my ways; violence is not the answer. Psycho played Harry Snatch. Well, Psycho, he was shot two days after me."

St. Peter spoke up,

"Kiely Angel you live up to your name. I am so proud to announce that you are now part of the Angel Defense Force.

I would like a special Angel to present you with your Angel wings."

Kiely and John's Dad appeared, holding a medal which is in the shape of wings and placing it over Kiely's head. He hugs both his lads,

"I love you both with all my heart."

St. Peter gets a message in his earpiece,

"God has just passed me an urgent message. He believes you can do this work as your former self.

He is giving you a second chance. God says to thank your mum and Celia, for their constant love and prayers. Don't worry you will always be part of the Angel Defense Force. God says you will continue your angel activities on earth. You must say goodbye to John and your Dad, they are always with you."

Kiely felt like he was flying down a spiral staircase; his body jolted and he opened his eyes.

Celia and Kiely's mum looked at Kiely, speechless as a miracle occurred. They saw Kiely open his eyes and look around the hospital room. Celia stood up and slowly moved to Kiely's bed.

"Love you, Celia. Love you.

There was a vicar in the room who was going to read Kiely's last rights, right there a miracle happened and the Vicar closed his bible and touched Kiely on his shoulder and left the room.

Kiely sat up,

"I have a second chance to live my life."

Alfred Lemon

It is 1810; a harsh winter in London's slums of the East End. Snow covered the terraced houses and roads. A man called Alfred was grieving. He had recently lost his wife and the mother of his only child. From the damp walls of the abode shared by many other families, consumption spread like a fire in dry grass.

The next day after burying his dear wife, Alfred and his teenage son Todd had no choice, but to return to their work on the docklands. The little money they earned was just enough to keep them alive.

As Alfred entered big wrought iron gates, all his workmates lined the entrance and paid their respects to both Alfred and Toby. Alfred was a proud man and saddened by the loss of his beautiful wife and the guilt of not being able to afford a good living for his family. He was the type of man you could depend on and would help anyone in trouble.

He was worried about his son Todd who had just started coughing, which he knew could be life-threatening.

"Todd; do you think you should go home today if you are not feeling well?"

"Dad I am fine honest; I will let you know if I am not feeling so good."

"I love you son with all my heart; you know that."

"I know Dad; you're a great bloke too."

Alfred worked in a different area of the docks than his son. As they separated, he looked at the red brick buildings and the cobbled road where Toby slowly disappeared into the distance. He felt so sad his son had to work, especially just after the loss of his mother.

Later that day Alfred heard a commotion and a lot of people shouting. Charlie one of his mates was sprinting towards Alfred. He stopped catching his breath.

"Alfred, come quickly; Todd has collapsed into the Thames."

Charlie still out of breath, pointed to where Todd had collapsed. With no hesitation, Alfred ran to the point in the Thames, took his hat off, and dived into the freezing Thames, rescuing his precious son.

Charlie and the Dockers gathered some blankets to warm Todd's frozen body. Someone has rustled up a horse and cart ready to take Alfred and Todd home. Charlie and the lads hoisted Alfred and Todd out of the freezing Thames and settled him on the cart. Alfred clung to his son, willing him to stay alive. Blankets were wrapped around them both. Charlie leapt on the horse and cart and cracked the whip. They travelled fast through the streets of London; Charlie knew this was an emergency. They could not afford to see a doctor and headed for Alfred's home in the slums of the East End. His house was shared with other families. Todd was now coughing nonstop. Alfred could not face losing another member of his family to consumption.

Charlie thundered through busy streets, pushing the horse to its limits. Alfred clung to his precious son and started praying for a miracle.

He kept repeating "I love you, my wonderful son."

"Dad, I love you. I can see Mum now, said Todd."

Todd gasped for air. It was his last breath. He lay in his dad's arms, his small thin body. He looked peaceful and felt so cold, his eyes closed in the arms of his dad. He passed away on the horse and cart.

Alfred cried and groaned like an injured animal. He looks up at the ceiling,

"No, not my precious son."

Charlie whipped the horse faster. They arrived back at their home in the slums of the East End. Alfred and Charlie carried Todd's frail body into the dark, damp room in the house. They placed him on some bedding on the floor and respectfully put blankets over him. Alfred kissed his son on the forehead. He fell to his knees and wept.

"I prayed for a miracle for my beautiful son. God has punished me. First my beautiful wife and now my beloved son. Those rich folk who lives in those big houses up on the hill; can afford to feed their dogs better meat, than I can afford. Rich people, with their servants and money to burn. I just wanted enough money to support my family and keep them healthy. It's time to get what my family deserves; my son deserves a king's burial. I'm going to tell those rich folk that they don't know how hard life is; for us working folk."

Charlie tried to stop Alfred,

"Please do not do anything stupid, you have had a big upset in your life. If you get caught you will end up in prison."

Alfred left the room angrily.

"A king's funeral I said."

Alfred began to run frantically up the hill, outside his home. Just in front of Alfred and up the hill, was an enormous large oak tree. As he got to the oak tree, a strange man behind the tree tripped him with his walking cane.

Alfred fell over and soon got to his feet and threw a punch. The man sidestepped the punch and said,

“Alfred, isn't it?”

“Do I know you?” “Well no, but my name is Kiely. I am very sorry to hear of the loss of your son Todd.”

Kiely was dressed in a seventeenth-century gentleman’s clothing, a white bouffant wig, a flintlock pistol, and a carved walking cane with a silver handle.

“Who are you, what do you want?” Kiely gently replied,

“I have been sent to help you, Alfred.”

“Listen Kiely, I don’t know what’s going on in your head, but I could just take you out at the moment.”

“Alfred, it was you who summoned me here today, when you prayed for a miracle? I suppose I am your guardian angel.

Did you know I can also travel back and forth through time? I have just been to the seventeenth-century shopping for clothes. These days, you know who (pointing upwards), is putting too much work on us Angels. Any way targets are not your concern.

Do you like my clothes? These clothes are the genuine article."

Alfred pushed past Kiely,

“You are crazy, now out of my way.”

Kiely grabbed Alfred's shoulder.

“I have been sent to help you! Listen, what if I could bring your son back to life again, I like that idea, don't you?”

Alfred stopped looking lost and empty.

“I would do anything to have my son back.”

Kiely took all his clothes off and stood naked,

“Listen, I know this seems strange but put on my magical clothes.”

Alfred was still in shock, but willing to try anything to help his son and decided to get changed into these strange clothes. Kiely placed the white bouffant wig on Alfred's head; he gave him a flintlock pistol and placed his magical cane in Alfred's hand. Kiely calmly explained,

"Listen carefully Alfie, you are going to the future where there is some medicine called antibiotics, got it? These antibiotics will save Todd's life, believe in me and Godspeed. By the way, it's a crazy world with lots of machines on wheels."

Alfred repeated several times

"Antibiotics, antibiotics, antibiotics." Kiely's voice started to fade into the distance,

"It will save your son's life, now get ready for your adventure."

There was a flash of light, and Alfred fell through a tunnel of light.

LONDON 2024

Alfred opened his eyes and was shocked by the noise of the busy traffic. He felt so scared seeing these machines on wheels, with people in. He kept reassuring himself.

"You are here for antibiotics."

Being scared, he decided that he was going to run for his life, across the road. A big red machine on wheels was steering towards him. He ran across a road, dodging the machines on wheels with people in them. Now across the road and panting heavily, he took a few quick breaths. He looked up to see a big silver machine in the sky, falling to the floor and covering his eyes with fear.

Onlookers avoided Alfred and walked around him, trying to not catch his attention. He looked up and saw an alehouse called the Park Tavern on Merton Road. He decided to go in and said to a man at the bar,

"Where am I?"

The man looked him up and down.

“You care in the community, geezer, or what?”

There was a group of lads singing and chanting in the far corner. Their chanting soon turned to Alfred, who was still dressed in his seventeenth-century clothing. Two lads came out of the mob and approached Alfred. They pushed him, calling him names.

“Not a full ticket, a sandwich short of a picnic, nutter, weirdo, a psycho in the community.”

Alfred felt threatened and reached for his pistol.

“Stop it, or I’ll blow your head off.”

Alfred pulled his flintlock pistol and fired above the lads' heads. Part of the ceiling fell to the floor.

“Shut your noise or else, you will lose your chestnuts.”

The two lads stood back shocked. One of the lads moved slowly towards Alfred and introduced himself.

“I’m Todd, bloody hell mate, you are crazy.”

The other lad also introduced himself,

“I'm Freebie Chas, for Charlie. We could do with a psycho like you for our Army. We are Chelsea and we are never going to be defeated.”

All the other lads copied the chant.

“We are Chelsea and we are never going to be defeated.”

Alfred relaxed,

“I'm Alfred Lemon. Army, are you fighting the rich for a better living?”

Todd grunted,

“Yeah, fighting for a better Chelsea; something like that.”

“Why are you called Freebie Chas?”

Freebie belched,

“I never pay for anything, so get us a pint.”

“I have no money.”

Todd was thinking they could do with Alfred in his mob.

“The drinks are on me, Psycho. We are in for a right battle today. Come on lads, let’s have 'em.”

Freebie went to the bar for Todd, to get Alfred a drink. Alfred slowly drank his pint, while Freebie Chas picked up someone’s drink and downed another man's pint.

Before Kick-Off

Todd led his men to Putney Bridge, South West London. They were going to fight the Portsmouth mob, led by Billy.

Alfred turned to all the lads,

"These rich sods, they throw food away, they have got servants, silk sheets. Yet we live in severe poverty and squalor."

Todd looked at Freebie and pointed to his head to make a crazy sign.

"I tell you Lemon, you are one crazy horse, eh Freebie?"

Freebie laughed,

"Yeah, Alfie's a quality psycho."

Todd led his men down the Putney Bridge towpath, where the Portsmouth mob were waiting. Todd gave the order,

"Let's have 'em. Come on Alfie, I want you to be my right-hand man."

Alfred ran into the angry mob with Todd and Freebie. There was a bloody fight, bottles, knives, and baseball bats. Alfred pulled his flintlock pistol and shot above the Portsmouth fans' heads. There was an instant silence, the stillness of the maddening crowds, followed by the noise of Police sirens.

Todd told his gang,

“Leg it back to the park.”

They got a tube to Southfields Station and made their way back to the Park Tavern pub.

PARK TAVERN

Todd laughed excitedly,

"That was bloody chocolate. We had 'em on the run. Alfred, you are a crazy lemon, you scared them out of their wits. Get the Lemon a drink."

Alfred felt proud. He stood on a chair in the Park Tavern and faced the gang.

"The battle is not over; they are probably regrouping."

The rest of the lads laughed. The next thing, a brick flew through the window and glass shattered over everyone. The Portsmouth mob rushed into the Park Tavern, fighting with Todd and his gang. There was another bloody battle; as two of the Portsmouth mob were kicking Todd on the floor. Alfred waded in and rescued him.

Freebie was nowhere to be seen. Alfred saved Todd from a right kicking and the Portsmouth mob legged it away as fists, and kicks hit them on the run. Freebie came out of the toilet.

Alfred looks concerned,

“Are you all right Todd?”

“Yeah, great mate, you are a diamond geezer Alfie. Do you fancy a Ruby Murray?” Alfred looked confused. Todd laughed

“Curry you Muppet.”

Alfred just nodded. They ran from the Park Tavern to the lad’s favourite curry house. When the food came, Alfred ate like a starving man. Todd passed his food to Alfie, as he had never seen a man eat so desperately. Freebie started to tuck into Alfie's food as well.

Todd told Freebie,

“Get your own, you tight git. Are you going on to a club?”

Freebie still tucking into the food, nodded.

Todd said,

“I'm going home, Alfie you need somewhere to kip?”

Alfred looked tired.

“I'm knackered; travelling through time is hard work.”

Todd's House

Todd and Alfred entered the house. Todd's Dad was sitting in his faded blue armchair watching Match of the Day. Around his feet were many empty cans of beer and a half-eaten Chinese takeaway. Alfie's bouffant wig caught his attention.

"Is he a queenie or what?"

Todd ignored his father.

Todd's dad got up and grabbed his son's throat and threw him to the ground.

"Is he a queenie or what?"

He went to kick Todd when Alfred intervened. Todd's dad got violent and threw a punch at Alfred. Alfred blocked the punch and pulled him to the floor. He wrestled Todd's dad and got him into a headlock.

Alfred angrily shouted,

“You are a disgrace; how could you treat your flesh and blood like an animal? You are lucky to have a great son. I lost my precious son.”

Todd's dad got up and left the house while slamming the front door behind him.

Todd apologized to Alfie. He realized he had never had a real father figure who was interested in his life.

“I'm sorry Alfie; you see violence is part of my life.”

“Are you really fighting the rich classes for a better life, to change things for the working man?”

“You must be stupid Alfie. We do it just for the kicks.”

Alfred felt ashamed.

“You mean it is mindless violence.”

“That's what working class lads do, isn’t it?”

Alfred looked at Todd,

“No, Todd. This mindless violence is wrong. You can change things for a better life. You're a great person; you can do anything if you put your mind to it.”

“I've always wanted to be a fireman.”

Alfred reassured Todd, well in the morning let us go to the fire brigade. Todd looked up the fire service recruitment centre. The next morning, Alfred kept to his word; they went to the Fire Fighter’s recruitment centre.

He reassured Todd,

“To fight fires takes real bravery, I am so proud of you for coming here today.

Todd smiled and asked Alfred,

“The other day Alfred you said time travelling was tiring, what did you mean?”

“You see, I am from the past. But there is something I need to ask you, Todd, it’s urgent. Can I ask you a big favour?”

“Yeah, what mate?”

Alfred said,

“I need to get some antibiotics, could you get them for me?”

Todd laughed.

“That’s no problem.”

He rang Freebie and asked him to get some antibiotics also.

Both lads made appointments the next day at the same doctor's surgery. The doctor prescribed them antibiotics after some good acting.

They both gave Alfred the prescriptions for antibiotics, that he had asked for. He could not thank the lads enough. Then there was a flash of light. The two lads were shocked as an intense light beamed on Alfred. Alfred's cane started to glow and vibrate.

He shouted,

“Live your dreams and follow your heart lads.”

1810 London

Alfred and Kiely were now back in the Smoke of old London. The London Alfred was used to. Somehow during the time travel, Alfred's correct clothes were now on.

Kiely stood in seventeenth-century clothing and said,

“We have returned to the day of your wife’s funeral. I will leave you now Alfred, run home and give the antibiotics to your son.”

Kiely disappeared.

“My wife’s funeral. That means my son is still alive. He’s alive.”

Alfred sprinted home and entered the grey crowded house. There sitting on a stall was Alfred's son Gareth. He was near his mum’s pauper’s coffin, in the damp room of their home. He hugged and kissed his son, jumping for joy.

“My wonderful son, you are alive. You know I love you with all my heart; I'm so proud to be your Dad.”

Gareth coughed.

“Dad, you are acting strange.”

Alfred held the antibiotics out and said,

“Gareth, you must take this medicine, one tablet every four hours, for one week.”

Gareth looked confused.

“I'm all right Dad and what’s this poison you want me to take.”

“Son, I beg you to start this medicine and I mean right now!”

After a week of giving him antibiotics, Gareth’s cough disappeared. Miraculously Gareth was still alive and made a great recovery.

Alfred started to teach all his docker friend’s new songs he had learnt on his magical adventure.

One evening down the pub everyone was singing,

"Blue is the colour and Chelsea is our name, we are all together and football is our game. So, cheer us on through the sun and rain because Chelsea; Chelsea is our name."

Alfred made a ball out of rags to play football. Alfred and Gareth played football with the other lads on Sunday afternoons. History was made, and the football fan was invented. Alfred loved his son so much that he managed to time travel to save his life. Albeit, with the help of a Guardian Angel.

Cat Agency

"My name is Charlotte and I am eleven years old. Me and my brother Daniel who is six; usually getting ready to go to Sheringdale Primary School. But today we have taken a duvet day, as Dad calls it. Because Mum has to take Nan to a hospital appointment."

I told Daniel that we are going to stay in our pyjamas and watch a film. Dad had made some popcorn to watch our film called Finding Nemo. We all got cosy on the sofa, watching the film, and munching on homemade popcorn. Daniel munched the loudest, shovelling hand falls of teeth like popcorn into his tiny mouth.

Just as the film was finishing Mum's car pulled into our drive. Daniel and I looked out of our bay window and waved at Mum. Mum got out first and slowly helped Nan out of her seat. Nan was wearing her brightly coloured red coat. It took Nan some time to get out of the car, Dad went to help Mum.

Nan steadied herself as she got out of the car. As soon as she saw Dad, tears started to roll down her red cheeks. He helped Nan into the house. Dad cuddled Mum and Nan as they entered the hallway. I stood up and went into the hallway and noticed both Mum, Nan and Dad were crying.

I started to cry too, but I didn't know why.

"What's wrong Mum, Dad, Nan?"

Then my brother came into the hallway, he too saw everyone crying. Mum, Dad and Nan came over and gave us both a big hug.

Nan put on a brave smile,

"First I need a cup of tea and a niece piece of chocolate cake."

Nan insisted on making everyone a drink and all of us having a piece of chocolate cake. She then sat next to me and Daniel.

She said,

"My wonderful Grandchildren, I love you both with all my heart. But the Doctor has said I have an illness. This illness is a bit like Pac-Man, which likes to eat the healthy cells, inside my body.

I looked at Nan, wiping the tears away.

"Do you me cancer Nan?"

Nan nodded,

"Yes, my lovely."

Daniel came over with his fists clenched,

"I could fight the Pac-Man Nan?"

Nan gave us both a cuddle and she just held us.

"There are a lot of things I want to do, in the next weeks with you all. I have written a list of the crazy and wonderful things we can do."

Nanny's List

Nan had written a list of things she wanted to do. The list was in her journal.

She called all the family into the lounge and said,

"This is my list of things I would like to do, are you ready?

1. Jam jar fishing at Wimbledon Park Lake.
2. I want to have a tea party with my amazing family every day.
3. I want to sit around a fire in the garden and tell stories.
4. Nan wants a tipple of Sherry every night.
5. I want to tell you all I love you, every night.

No time to waste let us do jam jar fishing."

Daniel went over to Nan,

"What's jam jar fishing?"

Dad smiled,

"You will find out soon. This takes me back to when I was little."

Nan described what to do,

"Put some stones in the jar, to make it sink to the bottom. You also add the bread into the jar before you drop the jar into the lake. Then you put some material with a hole in it over the jar and tie string around it, so the material does not fall off. Then the fish try to get the bread in the jar and you will catch several fish. You lift the jar to see what you have caught, then gently release them back in the lake."

Mum and Dad got the empty jam jars ready, they put some material over the jars. They made holes in the material so fish could enter. Dad secured the material on the jars with some string.

Wimbledon Park

It was a beautiful sunny day, Mum and Dad prepared a packed lunch. We parked in the car park and we all carried the buckets, nets, and the picnic hamper. Nan bought her folding chair and sat near the edge of the lake. She showed us what she used to do and lowered the jam jar with the bread and small stones into the lake. Within minutes she lifted the jar and two small fish were nibbling on the bread. Daniel and I were so excited. Nan gently released them into the water and passed the jars to me and Daniel.

Daniel and I excitedly lowered the jars into the water. I looked up at Nan, who beamed with a big smile. She gazed at us for quite a while. She saw how happy we were.

Then I pulled my jar up.

"Look everyone, I have caught two tiny fish."

I gently put the fish back into the water.

We sat on the picnic blanket, in the park, basking in the sunshine. Nan helped get all the food out of the hamper. As we had our dinner, Nan told stories about when my Dad was young. We all started laughing. Dad was quite naughty and misbehaved. After lunch, we all went for a game of mini-golf in the park. It was such good fun.

That night Nan had a tipple of sherry. Daniel and I both kissed her good night before we went to bed and told her that we love her.

Nan hugged both her grandchildren,

"Love you both forever."

Tea Party in the Garden

Mum had been up late through the night baking cakes for today's tea party. When we came downstairs, there were a lot of cakes on the kitchen table. Mum brought Nan a cup of tea up to her bedroom and sat with her until she was ready to get changed and washed.

Then they both came downstairs. Nan noticed all the cakes in the kitchen.

"Wow, they look scrummy yummy."

Nan hugged us both and said,

"I love you both with all my heart."

That morning, we all helped Mum make sandwiches and decorate the cakes. We had carrot cake, Victoria sponge, lemon drizzle, scones, and chocolate brownies. It was a beautiful sunny day, Dad put out a table and chairs, then laid a picnic blanket out on the grass fastened with tent pegs. Mum put a blanket around Nan, who stayed in her dressing gown for the first time. We all moved the sandwiches and plates onto the table in the garden. Then Dad slowly lifted the decorated cakes from the kitchen to the table in the garden. We all filled our plates full of yummy cakes and sandwiches.

Nan told stories of when she was young, as we ate. She told us that she used to play out in the streets and loved playing football with the boys. But back then girls were not allowed to play football. She remembered a magnificent goal she scored while playing in a park.

"You see in those days we did not have a football each. We all had to contribute our pocket money or get a paper round to help pay for the football. Sometimes we would even take pop bottles back to the shop, they would give us money for the used bottles."

I asked Nan,

"How old were you when you started the paper round?"

She smiled and said,

"I was ten years old. In those days it was normal for young people to get a job."

Daniel went up to Nan holding his football,

"Were you as good as me Nan?"

Daniel turned and tried to dribble with the ball.

Nan laughed,

"If there would have been an England Team for women, I would have been their lead striker. I could dribble, I could shoot from anywhere."

"I want to be a good footballer like you Nan."

Nan gently squeezed Charlotte's hand,

"Anything that you want to do is possible, with positive thinking and practice. But most of all, never give up on your dreams."

Mum asked Nan to talk about what it was like to be a young person during World War two.

Nan said "I was seven in 1944. My Dad, your great-grandad had to join the army. I can remember the sirens going off. We would have to make our way down to the tube station, with my mum, your great-grandma. We would all get a spot in the tube station and pick up some blankets and a cup of Cocoa. We would hear the whistling of the bombs and then explosions. We were all so scared."

Nan had a slurp of her tea.

"War is the most terrible thing. You see before the war ended in 1945, a policeman knocked on our door.

He handed my mum a letter and said how sorry he was. My Mum cried straight away, without opening the letter."

"What happened Nan," said Daniel.

Nan felt sad, these memories made her cry. Mum passed Nan some tissues.

Nan wiped her tears and blew her nose,

"The letter said that my Dad had been killed fighting in a battle. He had been awarded a bravery medal for saving his officer's life."

Nan talked about her life until late evening. No one wanted to move, just in case they missed something Nan was discussing. We all stayed with Nan until it was morning. Daniel and I were tired and we kissed Nan. Nan looked at us both and hugged us.

"I love you both so much and want you both to know, I will always be here for you. I don't want you to be sad if it's my turn to go to heaven, I know I will meet my mum and dad there. It would be brilliant to have tea and cake with them again."

Mum and Dad stayed up all night and they helped Nan to bed. That night Nan passed away and went to Heaven to meet her mum and dad.

That morning Mum and Dad looked sad; Mum had tears in her eyes. Mum came up to our room and gave us both a big hug.

"Love you Charlotte, love you, Danielle. Some sad news, that Nana has gone to Heaven."

There was a slight pause, and we all started to cry. We felt sad for a long time after, we thought Nan would come back in person and bring us some cake. We all felt such sadness at the loss of our wonderful Nan.

Nan goes to Heaven

Nan found herself at a hospital reception centre. There was a receptionist who told her to take a seat. Then this nurse with an old-fashioned nurse uniform, with a white hat and a black cape on, called Nan's name. Mrs. Fisher. Nan put her hand up and walked forward. The nurse took Nan to a small room.

She explained,

"You will need to have a check over. Then she will see all her loved ones who are in heaven. It will all seem confusing at first. After you have met your family, one of the Angels wants to ask you about our new service to help our families back on planet Earth."

Nan looked confused, and then her Mum and Dad appeared. Then her husband. There was a pot of tea and biscuits in the room. Nan hugged her Dad and cried, while Nan's husband poured the tea.

After a while, an Angel came to see her. She wore a bright white costume; her long feathery white wings were pulled into her side of the body. She had long dark hair and blue eyes. Her eyes were dazzling blue and she greeted and smiled at everybody in the room. She waved her hand and pointed to a television screen. With a wave of her hand, the screen came on. It showed that loved ones could be transformed into cats and sent back to planet Earth to support their loved ones.

Nan said,

“Each person was going back to their loved ones as a cat. I don’t get it.”

The Angle asked Nan,

“Would you like the opportunity to go back to your family and be around them?”

Nan still feeling confused,

“I love my family, and would do anything to be around them.”

The Angel smiled,

“What if you could return to your family on Earth, as a stray cat? Your family won’t be able to recognise you, but you would bring huge comfort to their lives.”

After months of being with her family in Heaven, Nan met with the Angel again.

“I am ready to go back to my amazing family as a cat.”

The Angel smiled and rubbed her hands together, sparkling gold dust fell from her hands to the floor, then a flash of light.

A ginger cat was meowing at the front door. Charlotte and Daniel opened the front door and the ginger cat came in. The cat just wanted strokes.

Mum said

"I wonder whose cat it is?

After several strokes, Dad put the cat outside, but it kept coming back to the front door and meowing.

Charlotte said,

Mum, Dad can we keep the cat? Oh please."

Dad said,

"This cat must belong to somebody; I will phone the vet and check with the neighbours if they have lost a cat. "

Mum phoned the vets and Dad went to ask the neighbours if they knew if anyone had a ginger cat.

Dad came back after an hour,

"No one is missing a ginger cat."

They put the cat into a breathable box and they all drove to the vet. The vet scanned the cat and could not find a microchip.

Dad asked the vet,

"Can we adopt this cat?"

The Vet knew Nan previously and nodded, that this cat would provide some comfort during their loss.

Mum smiled at the Vet,

"Can we have a microchip fitted with our details?"

The cat stayed all night. Charlotte and Daniel took turns reading Ginger a story. Every night Ginger would take turns sleeping on our beds.

The Screwdriver Brothers

It was 2012; two years have passed since the last election. The new coalition party condemned the previous government for their spending. They announced that cuts and job losses are the only way to free this country of debt. The working people of England are being brought down to their knees. Millions of working families have had their homes repossessed; charity organisations must lay on soup and food banks. It's a time when the building trade is at an all-time low.

Michael Flem was a Master Carpenter and joiner. His craftsmanship and reputation had made him successful; you would have to book him three years in advance. The recession was putting a strain on the building trade.

Michael always wanted children but was unable to have a family. Michael and his wife Margaret wanted to give two teenagers a home and a chance to help them get a joinery apprenticeship.

They went through a rigorous adoption process and finally found two teenagers whom they wanted to adopt.

Aubrey and Wandle were two normal 16-year-olds; with a good sense of humour. They both have a lot in common, even though they are not related. For the last ten years, they have been in care. Aubrey was of White British origin and Wandle was from Jamaican parents. Wandle would say,

"They were brothers from other mothers."

They were best of friends and their wishes had just come true. All the lads wanted was to be together, in a safe family.

Before the new parents arrived, the children's home manager Mary O'Rourke asked the lads to come to her office to complete the final paperwork. Mary was a tall, stern woman who took no nonsense. As she sat at her desk, the end of the desk fell away, bringing all her paperwork to the floor. The lads tried not to laugh. Mary shouted,

"It is you two who fixed my desk, admit it."

"No Miss, honest," they stated.

Mary looked them in the eye,

"Thank goodness you are going, and your fixation on dismantling things has run thin with me."

Mary double-checked the paperwork and waited for Mr and Mrs Flem to arrive.

The newly adopted parents were both excited as they drove up the shingled path to the children's home. They both exited the car and went to the reception area, where they were called into Miss O'Rourke's office. Aubrey and Wandle looked a little awkward when their new adopted parents, entered the office. The paperwork was finalized. The new parents loaded the car with the lad's suitcases. Aubrey and Wandle beamed with happiness as they waved goodbye to Mary. They got in the car and drove to their new home.

New House

Michael and Margaret welcomed the lads to their new home in Southfields, South West London. Michael took them upstairs and showed them his handiwork with the fitted wardrobes and their new bedroom. He thought it best that they share a room. The lads bounced on their beds and laughed with excitement and relief. They felt free for the first time in ten years. They both looked out of their bedroom window and noticed other lads playing football in a playground, not far from their back gardens.

They excitedly said to their new parents,

"Can we go over and play football with those lads?"

The Flems agreed. The lads were very confident and very skilful footballers. They introduced themselves and soon joined in the game of football.

They played football on a patch of triangle concrete, surrounded by houses on one side and flats on the other side.

From one of the flats, a rocker aimed his air rifle. Aubrey winced in pain as he was hit by the lead pellet. Wandle ran to his new parents and told them what had happened. Without delay, Michael ran around to the playground in his sandals. He helped his newly adopted son and checked his wound.

"Who did that, Wandle?"

All the lads pointed to the rocker's flat. Michael was furious and angry. He ran over and jumped into the rocker's garden.

"Come on then grease ball, let's have you."

But the rocker would not come and face the music. As Michael moved away from the flat; the rocker ran out and got on his motorbike and sidecar, driving off at speed.

Michael gave a pathetic chase in his sandals and waved his fist at the rocker. He took Aubrey and Wandle back home for their tea.

Over the next few days, Michael was busy with his portable screwdriver, fixing units in the lads' bedroom.

The lads watched their new dad with great enthusiasm, asking for a go on the screwdriver.

One evening, the lads decided to sneak out of their house with their new dad's portable screwdriver. They went to where the rocker lived. In a frenzied revenge, the lads dismantled the rocker's motorbike; outside his flat.

That morning the rocker came out dressed in his best teddy-boy suit, as he was getting married to his girlfriend who was pregnant. He wanted to put some white ribbon on the bike and sidecar to make it a special occasion.

As he opened his front door, he saw his bike in bits over the front garden. He exploded in a rage of temper. Explicit language could be heard across the estate. His pregnant bride came out of their flat with her motorcycle helmet on; to find her future husband on his knees crying.

Aubrey and Wandle watched from across the playground; they looked at each other and both said simultaneously,

“Revenge is sweet, bruv,” smiled Aubrey.

“Wandle laughed,

“Yeah, no one shoots my bruv and gets away with it.”

Aubrey and Wandle soon settled into their new life. They often liked to help their dad at weekends with his carpentry and joinery work. Michael could see the lads have a talent for fixing things and decided to buy them their own portable screwdrivers.

Comprehensive School

Aubrey and Wandle joined their local comprehensive school to start in the sixth form. They soon became very popular and made lots of friends. Like most teenagers, they were always playing practical jokes. For some reason, Mr Harris their Head of Year Teacher did not see eye to eye with the lads and was the brunt of their jokes. As he opened the door to his classroom, the door came crashing to the floor. Mr Harris soon followed. All the class laughed and kept laughing. Someone had removed the screws from the hinges. Mr Harris got up and shouted at Aubrey and Wandle,

"Up to the headmaster's room now."

Aubrey tried to explain,

"But sir, I."

Mr Harris did not let Aubrey finish, he sat at his desk when there was another crash-bang noise. Mr Harris's desk had now collapsed to the floor.

The class erupted with hysterical laughter. Mr Harris was knocked off his chair to the floor.

“To the headmaster’s office now!”

Outside the headmaster's office, the lads got their portable screwdrivers out of their rucksacks. They started to loosen the screws on the school award trophy cabinet.

As soon as the headmaster called them in, the trophy cabinet collapsed behind them.

The headmaster was livid;

“You two think your pranks are funny. This behaviour is not acceptable and I have decided to exclude you both from this school and sixth form.”

Our First Job

The lads were keen to become joiners; their fascination for portable screwdrivers was now going to become a reality. Michael bought the lads the latest portable drills and screwdriver attachments.

In their first job, they worked all over London. They were always playing jokes on the lads on the building sites, where they worked. They also went to the London School of Joinery and Carpentry, to get their City & Guilds qualifications.

The building trade was now falling on hard times and work was scarce. Soon all the wealthy reliable customers ditched their master craftsmen for cheaper, second-rate work.

Michael could not compete with cheaper tradesmen. He told his customers, that a cheaper price does not bring quality and craftsmanship.

The lads kept getting laid off from work. Michael Flem reassured them that things would pick up with their trade.

He could not sleep at night, worrying about where the next penny was going to come from. His adopted sons reassured their new dad; they were happy to work for nothing.

Michael felt devastated and a failure to his family. One evening the phone rang, it was his friend Bob.

“Hello Bob, what’s happening?

“I have got a big contract for the Tower of London and desperately need three joiners”

“You’ve made my day Bob; all three of us will be there first thing tomorrow morning. Once again, thanks mate.”

“No problem, Michael, I know I’ve got the best on the job.”

The Big Job

Michael and the lads turned up at the Tower of London with all their tools. Michael Flem was very proud that his adopted sons were following in his footsteps. Without delay, they started work; putting in twelve-hour days. It was a big job and would take a year to finish.

For some reason, after two months of work; the local authority who commissioned the work, decided to lay Michael and his lads off. The foreman delivered the bad news to Michael. He felt betrayed and angry. He had lost his livelihood to support his family and provide apprenticeships for his lads. Michael got the lads together and advised them of the local authority's decision. He tried to put on a brave face;

"Come on lads let's go for a pint.

He had a pint with the lads and gave them some money.

“I’m going to leave the van here overnight. I want to walk home to clear my head. If you could bring the portable drills home.”

“Aubrey looked at Michael in the pub,

“I tell you where the money has gone for that project; they have spent it on those expensive pieces of art for the Olympics.

It Started in the Boozer

The lads drank many beers and chasers. Aubrey and Wandle had that mischievous look in their eyes. With their small screwdrivers, they began to loosen the screws that supported the mahogany bar. They made their way around the pub, loosening the framework of the bar, pictures and anything that had a screw in it. They drank their last beers down.

Then all around them chaos happened, literally the pub fell apart. The lads quickly left as the pub was in chaos. The bar's wooden panels fell to the floor bringing all bottles and glasses smashing. People started to panic and were shouting at the bar staff.

Aubrey and Wandle laughed and an idea came to Wandle,

"Aubrey, I have had enough. We working people are constantly being screwed over. It is time to be creative and create work."

The Mission

That night they made history, as this was the beginning of an adventure to create work. The next morning every newspaper and TV news media reported that Tower Bridge had been dismantled.

Aubrey and Wandle dismantled Tower Bridge with their portable screwdrivers, like a shipwreck on the Thames. London became an unstable place and was put on high alert. The brothers made it their mission to create more work. In fact, for the next week, many of London's landmarks were dismantled. The news headlines, London under destruction, the lads went one further, dismantling Wembley Stadium and bringing it down to its grassroots.

The police had their work cut out, as the government cutbacks were affecting all investigations.

The brothers decided to leave, to go to France and Europe.

The more their handy work hit the news, the more people became curious. This led to a big following on social networks.

Europe

Michael Flem was worried, as the lads had not returned home. He also watched the news and said to Margaret,

"This destruction was terrible, but it will cause some jobs and employment. Who would do such a thing?"

Paris

Aubrey and Wandle had somehow managed to get to Paris, by paying with their credit card. They checked into a bed and breakfast and decided to go sightseeing in the evening.

Armed with their portable screwdrivers, they took in the Parisian sights. It was late and a winter's night. The lads could see their breath in the icy cold air. The lads had not prepared for the icy weather and looked a little out of place. They went to the Eiffel Tower; where they knew this was their next challenge. By late evening the now-adopted brothers sat under the tower. Wandle looked up from where he was sitting, to see this powerful metal structure.

"Let's do it Aubrey; take it down."

Aubrey sighed,

"Do you think this job is too big to do in one evening?"

Wandle laughed and got his portable screwdriver out,

"No way, this beast was for the taking."

He took a can of car paint out of his rucksack and sprayed screwdriver brothers on the ground.

Both lads worked themselves into a frenzy, soon bringing metal structures falling onto the floor. The tower's structural stability was now at risk; the lads continued further.

Aubrey noticed the unsteadiness of the tower and shouted,

"Leg it bruv, it's going to go."

The brothers grabbed their tools and ran for their lives. There was a quiet almost silent breeze, followed by a deafening noise of crashing metal. The Eiffel Tower was now dismantled and on the ground.

"You know we are in the deep brown stuff, Aubrey. You know we are not going to get a community service warning for this. Are you hearing me?"

Wandle could only stare at the gap in the sky; where the Eiffel Tower stood.

"We desperately need to get the hell out of here, where will we go?"

Aubrey scratched his head,

"Look, we were in big trouble anyway. Let's go for it and do it big. Let's create work around the world, how about Italy."

Both lads agreed as they revved their screwdrivers up.

Wandle smiled,

"Italia, home of good football and food, let's get the train from Paris."

The brothers moved on quickly to Italy via Paris. The next day all the French papers showed pictures of the devastation; France was in a state of shock and loss.

Italy

The brothers got off the train in Naples. They checked in at a bed and breakfast, where they stayed for one night. Somehow the brothers felt justification for their actions and believed in their mission to create work. They booked a trip around Naples. It is the last location on this trip that caught their eye.

There gleaming in the sunshine was the old King's palace in Caserta. The lads revved their screwdrivers and started to dismantle the old King's Palace. They could not help themselves as they dismantled the historic palace. Things were falling from ceilings and walls. Aubrey used the spray paint and signed the Screwdriver Brothers inside the palace. The staff in the palace ran around like headless chickens. Running all over, shouting at each other. The lads left, as the chaos unfolded behind them. The lads escaped back to Naples train station, where they brought their train tickets to Rome.

Rome

They managed to get their train to Rome, again checking in to a bed and breakfast.

This time they decided to go on their own and see the sights, armed with their portable screwdrivers. The lads managed to dismantle many buildings and bridges, leaving their signatures of spray paint Screwdriver Brothers were here.

That night, after pasta and many Sambuca drinks, the brothers boarded a train for Bologna. All the newspapers showed the destruction of well-known landmarks, with the sprayed identity of the perpetrators. Unknown to the lads there was a massive following on social networks for the Screwdriver Brothers.

In Bologna, they make their mark by dismantling the Leaning Tower of Pisa. This historical work of art came to the ground.

Aubrey grabbed Wandle,

"Let's go. It was now time to go one bigger and create loads of jobs in the USA. They stayed in a hotel in Bologna and booked their flights to the USA.

The lads checked the morning papers; the Screwdrivers Brothers were on the front page of the morning papers. The headlines read,

"Screwdriver terrorists bring down Europe's landmarks."

USA

The lads landed at Chicago O'Hare Airport. Aubrey turned to Wandle,

"Wicked, man, I can't believe I am in the Big Apple."

"Yeah bruv, this is the Country of Big. You will see some big jean sizes here mate."

They got into a taxi and wanted to go downtown. The driver was from Sierra Leone and did not know the way. The brothers read the driver's map book and directed the taxi to where Ernest Hemmingway grew up. They wanted to visit his landmark house and paid the taxi driver.

The lads checked into a motel and noticed a D.I.Y. store nearby. They decided to purchase the latest portable screwdrivers with their credit cards. They purchased the portable screwdrivers and went back to their motel to plan their mission. They turned on Sky News and to their astonishment, there was a picture of them wanted for dismantling Tower Bridge.

The Metropolitan Police was communicating with forces across Europe, for similar incidents.

The next day the brothers got a train into the city. They brought their portable screwdrivers as a precaution. On the train, they noticed areas that were run down.

They could not believe in this country of opportunity that there were such run-down shantytowns. Chicago's city centre was full of tall towers and a bustling city.

They toured around and visited the largest tower called the Hancock Tower. It was a thousand feet high and they decided to pay to go to the top. They could not believe that this monster of a building had two rooms only. The ground floor which you paid for, and the top floor to view the scenery. Yet while travelling on the train, there was so much poverty, that people crammed into shacks.

After going up the tower the brothers decided to help those people in those run-down areas.

They visited an Internet cafe and put messages on social media sites. It read,

"To the joiners of the world, we need your help. Please bring your tools; as we are going to build up the west side of Chicago. The place was run down and we needed to help the local people. We plan to start work in three days, see you there."

Aubrey said, "I can't see anyone turning up, can you bruv?"

Wandle laughed,

"What if thousands turn up?"

United Joiners

It was the day, to do some good work on the West Side; enthusiastically unplugging their charged screwdrivers. Eating toast and drinking coffee as they busied around their room. They headed for the train station with their tool kits. The train station seems packed with people with powered tools. The brothers and lots of people all got off at the West Side. There were thousands of people with boxes of tools, and hundreds of lorries, carrying timber, bricks, cement, and everything you would need to build houses.

These joiners had answered the brothers' prayers. Aubrey and Wandle were overwhelmed by the support of their fellow colleagues. The brothers stood on a platform and they addressed the eager crowd.

Wandle shuffled forward,

"Look around brothers, squalor in such a rich country.

How can the young progress, when crime was the only option of earning a good living? I thank you all for your help, United Joiners; I know we can make a difference."

It was at this point that all people united and showed kindness and compassion for others. They wanted to make communities better and create work. The thousands of joiners certainly did make a difference. All the houses looked like new houses. The police and mayor seemed confused. It hit all the major newspapers and media in the USA.

Every news programme showed the joiners united in their good work. Aubrey and Wandle had another big job to sort out. They asked the crowd for their assistance with the Hancock Tower.

Aubrey and Wandle shouted out,

"Brothers, we are all united as one screwdriver."

That day the tallest tower in Chicago got a major makeover.

The staff in the tower got overrun by joiners; the tower was packed with thousands of joiners working like ants in a colony. Then they could hear army helicopters above. The helicopters advised every joiner to leave the building or face serious consequences.

Aubrey and Wandle sneaked away unscathed. They left to go back to their motel.

“Where's next Aubrey?”

“How about getting a Greyhound bus to San Francisco?”

“Brilliant, let’s go, man.”

On the coach Aubrey says,

“While workers everywhere were fighting for survival; politicians and those at the top are getting richer. There were so many backhanders with the Olympics and so-called politicians; that we should just accept the corruption of the elite. Why aren’t these people investing in their communities; they are too busy lining their own pockets.”

"Me and you Bruv, feel enough is enough and we want to make a stand. I don't care if we are targets; we represent normal working people.

"They want us to be terrorists and be the bad guys. All we wanted was to work and a chance to earn an honest living."

Wandle nodded,

"You know we are both at risk of getting jailed or shot. I don't care what the consequences are; we are representing the working people and especially our poor dad. He has worked hard all his life and now he is out of work. Because he has some savings; he is not entitled to any help. What does this say about the country he has contributed to, all his life?"

Golden Gate

The brothers got to an Internet café in San Francisco and sent a message to all the joiners of the world.

"We just wanted to help people and create work. Please do not follow us further; as your lives will be at risk. We will be going to the Golden Gate Bridge today to surrender and make a speech of peace."

They arrived at the Golden Gate to find thousands of people from all walks of life. They all cheered and clapped when the brothers arrived. Both the brothers stood now on the Golden Gate Bridge. Police, the Army and every emergency service surrounded them. The Chief of Police called the brothers' names on a loud halo. With the Chief was their adopted father, Michael Flem. They asked Aubrey and Wandle to come forward, they moved forward anxiously.

Their adopted father Michael grabbed the halo,

"I love you both sons, and I am really proud, now run for your lives, they want you...!"

He did not finish his sentence as two shots were fired and then a barrage of bullets into the brothers. The crowd of joiners grabbed their screwdrivers and started to dismantle the bridge.

Thousands of other joiners came from the crowds, it was chaos. When Michael Flem ran out from the police to help his injured sons. A single shot was fired by accident and Michael fell to his knees with his arms in the air.

Aubrey and Wandle were still alive and got up to help their dad.

They held their dad in their arms. Michael looked up at them,

“I’m so proud of you both; for standing up for yourselves and against the odds.”

Michael gasped a last breath and passed away.

The brothers held their dad tight and wept, as a barrage of bullets from an army helicopter made sure both brothers were killed. Everything went quiet and eerie. The United Joiners laid their screwdrivers to the ground and surrendered.

Swim with the Fishes

Mafia boss Franco Russo was a notorious mob leader in the Cosa Nostra. He has a reputation to be feared. His mobster lifestyle had given him several spells in prison. In true mafia style, he took out anyone who got in his way.

Something strange was happening to Franco, he was starting to feel deep guilt about the bad things he had done in life. He was having nightmares about all the people he had killed; alongside the brutal violence he had implemented. He had started going to church more frequently and praying for forgiveness. Thirty-five years in the mob, makes a man's soul turn to concrete with the murder, violence, drugs, corruption, and hookers. He had seen it all and was now looking for retribution.

He wanted to make peace with his terrible world before he died. Franco would never show his men any weaknesses, as this would make him a target. He was old school and never asked his men to do something he would not do.

By personally whacking his enemies; he knew this would drive fear into his men.

His phone began to ring; it was his Captain Stefano,

“Boss got the main player; same as normal yeah.”

Stefano has captured that Roberto Taglia guy. Taglia and his mob had dealt on Franco’s turf. They were dealing drugs and undercutting Franco with their narcotics business.

Usually, anyone who double-crossed Franco ended up swimming with the fishes. He would normally take great delight in their execution. Franco always justified the violence as the Cosa Nostra Way.

He quietly said,

“It’s your call; look after the kid.”

Stefano was surprised,

“No problem got it covered; Rocco is a good kid.”

“Listen I don’t won’t Rocco doing any garbage, capice.”

“Boss no problem; but if he wants to be a made guy, he needs to get his hands dirty.”

“It’s not his time yet!”

"Okay boss, see you soon."

Franco was at a crossroads in his life, the guilt was now haunting him. He went into his bathroom and looked in the mirror. In a terrible rage, he punched himself in his face. He disliked what he saw and knew the change would make him and his family a target.

He started to prepare for this change; cash was handed over for a house in Syracuse. None of his mob was aware of this transaction. It was time to move his family there. Moving them to safety; ending this violent and criminal world. But this decision was going to put his life at risk for sure, time was needed to think. Franco planned a fishing trip to his hunting lodge on the river Lawrence. He needed this break to think things through and think about moving his family out of New York City, to Syracuse.

Stefano phoned Franco again,

"Boss I forgot, catch a fish for me?"

Franco's stomach churned,

"No problem, I trust you all the way."

Stefano laughed,

“Don’t worry he will be swimming with the fishes too.”

.

The Fishing Trip

Franco arrived at his hunting lodge near the river Lawrence. That night he made a log fire and downed a bottle of scotch. He soon fell into a deep sleep, surrounding himself with an array of weapons. He awoke startled and instinctively grabbed a gun. He quickly glanced at his Gucci watch, four AM. He heard a noise from the river. He could not work out if he was dreaming; as the most vibrant array of colours illuminated the sky above. That night, he saw a vision in the sky as clear as day. There above him were Heaven and Hell in the sky, light and dark. To the right of heaven, there was also a giant green hill. He stared at this vision for what seemed to be an eternity. Tears streamed down his face as he made the sign of the cross and prayed for forgiveness.

God spoke to Franco,

"There's one thing I need you to do. Please trust me. We are going under the water; you will be able to breathe as normal. This will be an emotional journey for you, but this will help you decide your destiny."

Franco listened and stepped forward into the cold wintry water. The cold shocked his body. He seemed surrounded by fish under the water, in which loads of fish started tugging at his clothing; soon pulling him under the murky river. All these fish pulled Franco under the river to a cave opening. The fish slapped Franco in the face with their tails, as they pulled him under the water.

One of the fishes called Pasquale waved his fin,

"Stu gatz, you killed me Franco. Yeah, you know who I am? I'm Pasquale."

Another fish introduced himself,

"I'm Rocky, you killed me and my brother. My kids were left without a father."

All the fish spoke and told Franco how he had killed them.

Rocky laughed,

"We have been swimming with the fishes since. Franco, you have been a bad man, it's time to do some good.

This was a warning to you, turn a new leaf. All the guys are willing to forgive you, if you turn a new leaf, Franco. "

Franco was confused and tearful.

"I have got blood on my hands."

He found himself floating to the top of the river; crying uncontrollably, coughing and spluttering, as he struggled to the bank.

God spoke to Franco,

"I and all of us in heaven believe you can change and do the right thing. I will be with you all the way."

Franco sat on his knees looking up at the sky and wiping his tears,

"Thank you, God; I won't let you down."

He packed his fishing stuff up and got into his jeep to drive back to New York.

Doing the right thing

There was a young kid Rocco Maggio, who loved Franco like a father. He wanted Franco to make him a made guy. Franco could see himself in Rocco and kept the kid under his wing.

Franco and his wife Immaculata invited Rocco and his girlfriend for a meal. Franco's wife Immaculata cooked the best meat and Brea Saola sauce in the world. They sat and ate five courses of food. Franco toasted Rocco and his girlfriend with Strega; "cento anni Rocco."

Franco wanted Rocco to live for a hundred years. After the meal, Franco took Rocco into the games room to shoot some pool. He spoke softly,

"Rocco, I treat you like my own son. But you know, what we do, who we are. It's a terrible business. I can never sleep at night because I have killed many people. Those people whom I have killed; have left their loved ones to pick up the pieces; this is my fault. Capice? What I am saying Rocco, I want you to have a better life.

You are a good smart kid. I want to help you move away from this and make an honest man of you."

Rocco looked up at Franco,

"I respect your good advice, but I still want in. I want to be a made guy, I can't do a nothing job."

"If you respect me; you will listen to my wisdom. Things are going to change for the better."

"You are like a father to me, but it still doesn't make sense."

"I have seen the light kid and the error of my ways. I want you out of this terrible business. People want me dead Rocco, I don't want you to be in this position. You see Rocco, I have seen the light. I have never seen it so clearly. Soon my men will make me their hit and Stefano will probably get you to do his dirty work."

"Boss, there is no way the guys are going to whack you. You are too respected; you and Stefano go back a long way."

"You have a very green view of this business. You have to lead with a gun covering your front and back.

You must be on guard twenty-four-seven, is that what you want for your girlfriend and future wife."

A Made Guy

Franco felt good about changing his life. He set out straight away to anonymously help all the families he had destroyed. He gave his men extra pay for being good. Franco decided the time was right to move his family to Syracuse, for safety. He also started volunteering at charities in New York, helping in soup kitchens and helping young people in rehabilitation. Franco was putting big money into social and community projects. Unfortunately, he was becoming very unpopular with his men and the word on the street was that Franco had lost his marbles.

He gave bonuses to his men; when they helped people. Meanwhile, Pasquale Gratto and his New Jersey mob were taking all of Franco's narcotics, gambling business, and building contracts. Franco was happy about this. Happy to get rid of his dirty laundry. Franco gave his men regular talks about how bad drugs were and that this was no longer good business. His men were angry and, in an uproar, they were losing business and the cash to feed their fat habits.

Stefano Mastro-Giovanni (Franco's right-hand man) calmed the men and gained the status quo. Franco of old would have punched a few faces for their uproar, but he just laughed at them. His men were plotting behind his back. Stefano wanted to be the boss and was orchestrating Franco's departure from this world. There is no such thing as Loyalty in this business; especially when the boss was soft in the head. It was Stefano's destiny and his time to be Don of the New Yorkers.

Every new kid or family member; who wanted to be part of the mob; Franco talked the younger generation out of it. He paid them to have a better education, or he would pay them to travel the world. The business was being lost; Franco was losing his reputation. New Jersey mobsters were now laughing at Franco and his reputation.

Stefano decided enough was enough. He pulled Rocco to one side.

He said,

“To be a made guy, you got to have a hit under your belt. I need you to whack a big gun. That’s all you need to know. Just do it, okay, capice?

Rocco replied,

“Capice.”

The Hit

Stefano arranged to meet Franco at Grand Central Station alongside the new kid in the mob, Rocco Maggio. Today was Rocco's initiation to be a made guy. To be a made guy; you must have a hit under your belt. Rocco was given the job of hitting Franco. This was Franco's final destiny. They met Franco on a platform at New York Central.

They all hugged and Franco said,

"I don't want this type of life any more. I know what's coming Stefano. I thought you were my family and friend."

Stefano gives Rocco the nod,

"You gotta be kidding, I can't whack the boss."

"You are a good kid; you don't need to do this."

Rocco was angry.

"Shut up see, or else."

Rocco panics and starts to run away, Stefano shoots his gun, four times.

Rocco hears the shots and turns back. Franco was lying on the floor, in a pool of blood. Rocco ran back to Franco and held him close.

Franco whispered,

"Bless you, son, make good of your life."

He pointed to an envelope in his coat pocket.

"You must leave here and live a good life. God really exists."

Franco died by the gun, in Rocco's arms.

The envelope contained a key and directions to his safe deposit box. Rocco took Franco's advice and moved away to Europe. His life changed at that moment, as he became a teacher and family man. Rocco and his wife raised two good kids and lived an honest, peaceful existence. He even named his son, Franco.

The Adventures of Danny and Uncle Phil the Space Pirate

It was the day before Christmas Eve, in Wandsworth London. Something adventurous was about to happen to an eleven-year-old boy called Danny. Although Danny lived with his Grandparents and his mum Rosie, this was no ordinary family. His Granddad and his Uncle Phil were both Space Pirates. Their job was to police space and the vast universe.

It was very cold outside; snow started to fall and settle on the street. Danny went downstairs and opened the curtains. Something caught his eye; it seemed like a cylinder shape was coming fast towards his house. He closed his eyes and when he opened them there was a huge purple space pirate ship, above the house. Not just any space pirate ship, but it was Uncle Phil's ship, called Loveness.

Loveness was a beautiful ship, her purple colour flowered the skies. This huge ship manoeuvred so easily and made light work of parking in the air, outside Danny's terraced house, in Wandsworth.

Uncle Phil looked like a pirate. He had a patch over his right eye and a big ginger beard. He gave the command to his colleague Tattoo Jack, who was a ginger cat.

A ginger cat that could speak hundreds of different languages, from English to Martian.

"Get ready to beam down to my Mum's house," said Uncle Phil.

Uncle Phil stood next to Tattoo Jack. Loveness sent a white beam of light over them, in which they disappeared and transported themselves down into the front room of the house. Danny's Grandma and his Mum Rosie were there too. Everybody was so pleased to see Uncle Phil and Tattoo Jack. Uncle Phil's Mum hugged both Space Pirates and said,

"I am so happy to see you both. Let me make you your favourite breakfast."

Uncle Phil smiled,

"Brilliant Mum."

"Where was Dad Phil, "said Mum?

Uncle Phil lowered his head,

"Mum, Dad volunteered for a special mission. He has volunteered to fly into a black hole, to see if he can find a way to time travel. If Dad can find a way to travel back or into the future, this will be the most amazing discovery ever."

Grandma did not share her son's enthusiasm. She had a tear in her eye as she looked at Danny.

"Why has he risked his life at Christmas time? We need him home. He promised Danny, he would be home for Christmas."

Uncle Phil looked at Tattoo Jack, who was cleaning his paws. Tattoo Jack looked at his adopted Mum. He went over and started to lick her hand. Grandma stroked Tattoo, who had got his name from having butterflies tattooed on each paw.

Tattoo purred and said,

"Grandma, Grandpa has been so brave. If he can work out how to time travel, he would use time travel to help the world be a more peaceful place."

Right then, a red buzzer alarm went off on Uncle Phil's watch. He had got an urgent call on his watch, from the Space Station. He answered,

"Yes sir, what! The Hungalian's have declared war on Christmas! They plan to kidnap Santa Claus? Sir, we are missing Grandpa and are now one person down."

Uncle Phil looked at Danny.

"Leave it with me, sir, I know my nephew Danny would be ready to help out."

He clicked off his watch.

"Did you get all that, Tattoo?"

Tattoo was cleaning himself.

"I can't believe the Hungalian's want to destroy Christmas and kidnap Santa. Those guys are just jealous because they don't have the magic of Christmas in their lives."

Uncle Phil turned to his sister Rosie,

"We need Danny to help us. We are short staffed and without Danny, well Christmas may be lost for now and possibly forever."

Danny looked at his Mum and then at Grandma.

"Pretty please, you know it's all I have ever wanted was to be a Space Pirate."

Rosie looked at Grandma,

"It's very dangerous up there. If anything was to happen to you, I would never forgive myself."

Danny looked at Uncle Phil and Tattoo,

"You will look after me, won't you."

Uncle Phil saluted,

"Aye, we will Danny."

Tattoo meowed,

"I can't wait to fit you up with the latest Space Pirates gadgets."

Rosie took one more look at Grandma, who nodded.

"It's decided then, you can go with all our love and blessings."

Danny hugged all his family and Tattoo Jack. He put some milk in a bowl, for Tattoo. He looked up at his family.

"What about Granddad? Will he be back soon?

Uncle Phil put his arm around Danny,

"Grandpa has gone on a very dangerous mission. We don't know if he will return."

Danny looked at all his family,

"He will return. Grandpa always said no matter how bad things get, never ever give up hope."

Breakfast

Grandma cooked sausages, eggs, bacon and rounds of toast and a pot of tea. She smiled,

"Who would have thought that Uncle Phil and Danny would follow in their Grandpa's footsteps? He would be so proud of all of you."

After breakfast, Uncle Phil and Tattoo helped wash the dishes. Uncle Phil turned to Tattoo Jack,

"We will have to go soon. You will need to get Danny ready for space travel. While you are doing all that, I must see our neighbour Mrs Jenkins. As I have got her some Martian fudge, the stuff that makes you younger."

Tattoo smiled,

"Ahh rejuvenating fudge. How old is Mrs Jenkins?

"About eighty."

Tattoo Jack measured Danny with his watch gadget and then pressed a button. A message was sent to Loveness, who produced him a Space Pirate flying suit. At the press of a button on his watch, the silver space suit appeared.

Tattoo Jack was so excited as he passed the suit to Danny.

"Here's your Space Pirate watch Danny. It can do millions of things. It can also transport you to Loveness or transport you anywhere in space or the world. You can even order your favourite food with this watch and Loveness makes it appear in front of you."

Danny went to his room to try his Space Pirate suit on. It fitted perfectly. He put his new watch on and tried the transport button. Speaking into his new watch, "Loveness transport me to the kitchen."

Unfortunately, he was transported into his neighbour's kitchen. They looked at Danny, as they rubbed their eyes with disbelief. Danny quickly spoke into his watch, "Transport me to my kitchen."

A flash of light and he was back in his kitchen.

"You look brilliant Danny."

Tattoo Jack produced a small device from his watch gadget.

"This small laser pen is used on your hand to protect you in space. A bit like when you get an injection to prevent diseases."

Danny braced himself, but he did not feel any pain. Tattoo gave him a piece of space gum.

"This gum would give you ten years of oxygen supply, so there was no need for a helmet or an oxygen tank in space."

Uncle Phil ordered drinks for everybody on his watch, a shot of rum for all the adults and milk for Tattoo and Danny. The drinks appeared.

"A toast to my good family, to our family."

Rosie smiled and raised her glass.

"To our family."

Everyone hugged each other. Rosie and Grandma gave Danny a big kiss. The Space Pirates pressed the transport button to Loveness. With a flash, they disappeared onto the Space Pirate ship. Danny looked out of one of the portal windows, he saw Mrs Jenkins jogging down the road.

Space

Loveness, was a beautiful ship, amazingly spacious and with comfortable furnishings. The ship even had a cinema room. Danny could not believe how big the ship was on the inside. Loveness welcomed him aboard.

"Hello, Master Danny, I have prepared you a hot chocolate with marshmallows. After you have had your drink, I will take you through your health and safety training. I will cover everything a Space Pirate will need to know."

"Wow, many thanks Loveness."

After Danny finished his drink, Loveness produced a virtual pair of glasses and demonstrated possible problems in space. As soon as Danny had passed his space pirate health and safety course, Uncle Phil gave the command.

"Let's head for the Hungalian planet."

Tattoo Jack reminded Uncle Phil,

"This will be a dangerous mission. You know the Hungalian's want to kidnap Santa and destroy Christmas."

Uncle Phil reassured everyone,

"Firstly, we find out as much information about the Hungalian's. Tattoo Jack, do you want to do your stuff? Danny and I will head for the North Pole, to protect Santa."

Danny swallowed hard,

“What if they try to attack us?”

Tattoo Jack smiled,

“Its ok Danny. I have magical powers and I can change into any person or shape. I can also speak fluent Hungalian. I will be transported onto the planet and will go undercover.”

Danny was excited as this was his first space adventure,

“Uncle Phil, Tattoo Jack and Loveness, this was the best day of my life.”

Loveness counted down,

“Ten, nine, eight, seven, six, five, four, three, two, one.”

They blasted off into space, at the speed of light.

Uncle Phil explained to Danny,

“The space gum Tattoo had given you would also stop you from floating around.”

“That is amazing Uncle Phil. “

Tattoo Jack and Loveness pointed out star patterns, solar systems, and planets to Danny. They whizzed through space at a supersonic speed.

Danny looked out of one of the portal windows, he saw a tiny planet of green and blue, called Earth. They travelled at electrifying speed, through the vastness of space.

Loveness put on the protective shield. She warned everyone,

"We will soon be invisible to the eye."

Tattoo Jack said,

"We are nearing planet Hungalian. I will soon need to transform into a Hungalian and be transported onto their planet."

Uncle Phil said,

"Do you want us to come with you?"

"No, your red beard will give us away."

Tattoo turned into a giant snail. Danny could not believe his eyes.

"Are Hungalian's, snails?"

Uncle Phil smiled,

"Yes, they are. Danny, are you ready to go and visit Santa at the North Pole?"

"Ready and excited Uncle Phil."

Tattoo Jack, now a snail produced a lot of slime and tried to hug Uncle Phil and Danny. He then beamed down onto planet Hungalian.

Uncle Phil asked Loveness,

"To the North Pole."

Loveness responded,

"Straight away Uncle Phil."

North Pole

Loveness headed at full speed through the Earth's atmosphere, to the North Pole. She then announced that she has received a text from Tattoo Jack, it read,

"I have landed. I am surrounded by giant snails and slugs. I will not contact you until I find out the Hungalian plans."

While Loveness was travelling at vast speeds through the universe, Uncle Phil was teaching Danny how to fly the ship and how to maintain the course.

Loveness announced,

"We are entering Santa's air space."

To enter the North Pole Airspace, Uncle Phil needed to enter a special code. This code was only known by Santa and the Space Pirates. He entered the code on his watch.

Santa's face appeared on the big screen. "Ho, Ho, Ho guys. I welcome your ship and give you permission for Loveness to Land."

Uncle Phil smiled,

"Yes sir."

Danny could not believe that the real Santa was on their big screen and touched the big screen.

Santa's Grotto

Santa Claus met Uncle Phil and Danny on the snowy landing strip. He had his sleigh and reindeer ready to give Uncle Phil and Danny a lift to his home.

"My wife has prepared us a meal. I hope you are hungry guys."

Uncle Phil said,

"I'm blooming starving."

Danny nodded, he tried to speak but he was so star-struck, he could not get his words out.

Santa patted Danny on the head,

"You must be really brave like your uncle and Grandpa, to be a Space Pirate."

Danny replied,

"I have always wanted to be a Space Pirate. I just want to help people like my Grandpa and Uncle Phil."

Santa smiled,

"You will do my lad, because you have a brave heart."

Santa gave the orders to the reindeer and off they flew into the air.

Santa gave them a tour of the North Pole and pointed out the Elves' village and the factory where all the presents are made. They landed outside Santa's house; it was all lit up with thousands of lights like stars shining so brightly. It was next to the gigantic factory, all lit up with thousands of coloured lights.

It was where they made all the toys and presents for the whole world. Danny could see many Elves going into the factory, whilst singing Christmas songs.

Mrs Claus came to the door and she welcomed everybody inside. She had red cheeks and white hair and her welcoming smile, made us feel special.

"Lovely to meet you."

Danny shook Mrs. Claus's hand,

"This must be a dream, being at the North Pole, with Mr and Mrs Claus. It's the best thing ever."

Uncle Phil agreed,

"This is so amazing."

"Make yourself at home," smiled Mrs Claus.

"After our fantastic tea, cooked by my good wife, I will show you around the factory."

Danny beamed with happiness,

"Do you mean I will get to see the factory?"

"Yes," Santa smiled.

Uncle Phil said to Santa,

"The reason for our visit was that we have some bad news."

Santa's face looked concerned,

"Is someone trying to spoil Christmas?"

Uncle Phil nodded.

"Yes, the Hungalian's want to kidnap you and destroy Christmas."

Santa scratched his white beard,

"But why?"

"The Hungalian's want to stop the magic of Christmas and they also want to take you hostage. In addition, they want you to deliver Christmas just for them and sell the North Pole for good."

Santa knelt next to Danny,

"If there is no Christmas, then children like you all over the world will be affected."

Uncle Phil said proudly,

"That's why my brave nephew and the Space Pirates are here, to help you, Santa. I will quickly demonstrate what we are up against."

Uncle Phil pressed a button on his watch. A screen appeared on Santa's wall and showed the short film showing the Hungalian's aliens.

Santa was horrified, as he looked at the giant snails and slugs.

"The Hungalian planet does not look like a cold place; in fact, it looks like there is a lot of rain. The jungle looks overgrown with plants and trees."

This film was sent by Tattoo Jack, who was undercover. After the short film, Mrs Claus announced

"Tea was ready."

Santa was still scratching his beard.

"How will we prevent the Hungalian's from destroying Christmas?"

Uncle Phil had a drink of some rum that Mrs Claus had provided.

"Once we get the intelligence from Tattoo Jack, we will work with you Santa, to make a plan."

They ate their tea and Santa arranged for some of the Elves to show Danny around the factory. Uncle Phil stayed behind as he needed to talk to Santa. The little Elves patted Danny on his head.

One of the Elves smiled,

"We are so pleased to meet you, Danny. Did you know Keith and I have been in charge of making your Christmas presents since you were a baby?"

Santa's Factory- 2 Nights Before Christmas

A snail appeared on Uncle Phil's wrist phone. It was Tattoo Jack.

"It's me, Phil, I have to speak quickly. They are planning to invade the North Pole on Christmas Eve. They have six fighter ships with the latest weapons."

Uncle Phil was concerned,

"Are you ok Tattoo, do you need backup?"

Just then Tattoo Jacks's disguise failed. He appeared as his cat self.

Uncle Phil quickly said,

"Disguise identity failed. We are coming to get you."

Then Uncle Phil saw that Tattoo was set upon, as giant snails surrounded him and took him away into the undergrowth. Uncle Phil pressed the alert on his watch, which sent Danny a message. While Loveness fired up the emergency ship. Uncle Phil transported Danny back to Santa's house. Danny looked shocked,

"What's up, Uncle Phil?"

Danny, I must go and rescue Tattoo. I want you to stay here and protect Santa. I'm going to get Tattoo Jack."

Danny looked sad,

“What happens if you don’t come back?”

“I will be back Danny, I promise. Once I am up in space. I will activate a salt invisible force field around the North Pole. Let’s face it snails and slugs do not like salt. I will give you access to all the functions on my watch.

I won’t be taking Loveness, as I will be going in the rescue ship, as it is faster and can’t be picked up on the radar.”

Santa Claus put his hand on Danny’s shoulder.

“Everything will be okay. I believe in you Danny and know how brave you are.”

Danny stood tall,

“My Granddad always said no matter how bad things get, never ever give up hope.”

Uncle Phil cuddled his nephew and beamed up onto the emergency spacecraft. The craft shot off at high speed into space.

Christmas Eve Morning

Danny was helping Santa and the Elves prepare for the greatest magical day of the year. Then Loveness contacted Danny.

"The salt protection in the atmosphere was not working and I have lost communication with Uncle Phil. What should we do Danny?"

Danny scratched his head.

"There was only one person who can help us. Grandpa."

Loveness responded,

"It's too dangerous Danny."

"I have no choice to go and get Grandpa if we are to save Uncle Phil and Tattoo Jack. He will know how best to tackle this problem. We must never give up hope."

"Let's do it, Danny." Loveness revved the engines.

Danny went over to Santa Claus and explained the situation.

"I have to go and rescue Grandpa, if we were to save the magic of Christmas."

Santa smiled,

"I am very proud to meet someone so brave. I believe you can do this Danny. I have a special gift for you."

It was a reindeer bell on a necklace. Danny put on the necklace.

“Thank you, Santa.”

Santa said,

“This is no ordinary bell; it is a magical bell that gives you one wish.”

Get Grandpa

Danny beamed up onto Loveness. She prepared Danny on what to expect as they entered a black hole. At the speed of light, they shot off into space. Danny was nervous and excited, as this was the greatest adventure ever. Loveness made Danny a drink of hot chocolate.

She then told him,

"We all believe in you, Danny. Don't worry about the black hole, I know I can work out a way to enter the black hole."

Danny looked worried,

"Thank you Loveness. Grandpa was the most amazing person ever; I don't know what I would do without him. I hope he was okay and we can find him?"

"We will do our best, Danny."

Danny could see the black hole on the big monitor.

Loveness advised,

"We will soon be approaching. Apply your safety belt, Danny."

They entered the black hole at a very fast speed. At first, it was a rocky ride. Loveness was being knocked from side to side.

Then there were some small explosions and a flash of light. Danny held onto the reindeer bell that Santa gave him. He made a wish.

“I wish to find my Grandpa.”

Then a bright tunnel of light appeared as they flew into it. They flew side to side, spun upside down and around like clothes in the washing machine. Then everything seemed silent and calm as they landed. Loveness checked her computers.

“Danny, we have landed in the past. We landed in 1940 London during the Blitz of the Second World War.”

“Loveness, do you think Grandpa was here?”

“Yes Danny, I am ninety-five per cent certain.”

Danny undid his safety belt and kissed the reindeer bell.

“Loveness, can you dress me in the clothes of this era? I need to leave you and find Grandpa.

Loveness soon transformed Danny into clothes for this era and provided him with a gas mask.

“I will have to make myself invisible and I will contact you via your watch.”

“Thanks, Loveness.”

London 1940

Danny left Loveness and entered the streets of London. It was daylight. Although people were getting on with their daily lives, he could see people in uniform trying to clear debris from a blown-up building. Danny went up to the men in uniform and showed them a black-and-white picture of Grandpa.

One of the men said,

"He looks familiar son. Is he a relative?"

Danny nodded,

"He is my Grandpa."

The man said,

"Where can I contact you, if I see him?

Danny had to think quickly. He gave his Grandma's house address. As she had told him, her Great-Grandmother lived in that house during World War Two. The man in uniform wrote it down. Danny decided to walk around London. There were a lot of people in uniforms. So many streets had been bombed. People seemed so brave, as they were trying to live normal lives. Kids were even playing on the rubble of the derelict building, that had also been bombed.

Siren Raids

It was now the early evening of December 1940. It was getting dark and all windows in the buildings had been blacked out. There were no street lights, as the air raid alarm went off across Wandsworth. Danny was not sure what to do. A warden pointed to Danny, to head for Southfields tube station.

Danny was scared and ran towards the train station. He could hear aircraft above and saw flashes of explosions. As he entered the tube station, a man was singing Beatle Songs to lots of people. It was Grandpa.

Danny ran to Grandpa and threw his arms around him. He could not hold back the tears. Grandpa was shocked.

"Danny is that you? I can't believe it. You never gave up on me. You are one special Grandson. I think the mission has been a success. I have found the particles that will allow us to time travel. I followed Einstein's theory and he was right you know. My ship was destroyed on entry into the black hole. This meant I could not leave this era unless someone special rescued me."

The surrounding people looked confused, as they did not understand what Grandpa was saying.

"Grandpa, Loveness was nearby. I am so pleased you are alive. We need to go as Uncle Phil and Tattoo Jack are in trouble. You see the Hungalian's want to declare war on Christmas and kidnap Santa. Tattoo Jack went undercover and now has been taken, hostage. Then Uncle Phil has gone to rescue him."

"Wow Danny my boy, a lot has happened since my mission. Don't worry son, we will rescue Phil and Tattoo."

They both ran up the stairs of Southfields tube station. Danny's watch was guiding them to Loveness. Bombs fell whistling onto the buildings of London.

Danny spoke to Loveness via his watch,

"Fire up the engines sister, I have found Grandpa."

"Brilliant Danny, will do," said Loveness calmly.

Rescue Christmas

Loveness shot into space. She gave Grandpa a shot of rum and made Danny a hot chocolate.

Grandpa cuddled his grandson.

"You are a hero. I am so proud of you Danny. You rescued me, under enemy fire. You never gave up no matter how bad things got."

Danny looked at his Grandpa,

"You are too special to lose."

Grandpa asked Danny and Loveness lots of questions about the Hungalian's regarding Uncle Phil and Tattoo Jack's situation. Once he had all the information, a plan appeared in his mind. It was like a light bulb had lit up above his head.

"You see the problem here is that the Hungalian's are jealous as they don't have the magic of Christmas. What if I could convince Santa Claus, to deliver the magic of Christmas to the Hungalian's? I know an old Hungalian elder and he knows me well. I will suggest it to him."

Granddad asked Loveness to send a message to the elder called Bryan.

The message read,

"We do not want any wars or violence. I have a solution to Christmas. What if Santa Claus can also deliver to you on Christmas Eve? Would you stop the war on Christmas and release my son and Tattoo Jack?"

Danny and Grandpa waited nervously for the reply. It came back straightaway and read,

"We do not want to fight over Christmas too. We accept your offer and can't wait till Christmas Eve. Uncle Phil and Tattoo Jack will be released soon, Merry Christmas, from Bryan."

Danny asked Loveness to contact Santa. Santa appeared on the big screen.

"Hello Grandpa, I am very pleased to see you again. I see that Danny has been really brave in rescuing you."

Grandpa smiled,

"Hello again to you Santa Claus. Danny is a true hero and deserves his place as a Space Pirate. Now I need a big favour to save Christmas. Do you think you could deliver presents to the Hungalian children, every Christmas? We would help you of course."

Santa Claus laughed aloud,

"Ho, Ho, Ho. Of course, I will the magic of Christmas is for everyone. However, I will need your help and Loveness to get everything completed on Christmas Eve?"

Just then Uncle Phil and Tattoo Jack beamed aboard Loveness, with flashes of light around them. Granddad and Danny hugged Phil and Tattoo. Loveness produced a shot of rum for the adults, milk for Tattoo and another hot chocolate for Danny.

The Space Pirates raised their glasses to Santa.

Grandpa gave the order,

"To the North Pole, Loveness."

Christmas Eve

The Space Pirates worked with Santa Claus and all the Elves. Santa thought it best to deliver to the Hungalian's first, as they were light years away. The Space Pirates took Santa, Elves, and the presents into Loveness. They worked non-stop. After delivering presents to all the Hungalian children, their elder leader sent a message of thanks and peace.

The Space Pirates then helped the Elves with all the presents for the children on Earth. But before Santa left, he asked Danny to sit on the Santa throne. All the Elves had stopped work and came into the courtyard, where Danny was sitting. Santa stood and put on the microphone,

"This award is the highest award for bravery and for not giving up, no matter how bad things got."

He put a medal over Danny's head and everyone cheered. Danny was so pleased, his smile beamed across the North Pole. Loveness sent a message for all the Space Pirates to board the ship.

Grandma and Rosie had been contacted with the good news and wanted everyone home for a family Christmas. All the Space Pirates pressed their watches and beamed up to Loveness.

Grandpa shared his dangerous mission.

"My mission was a success. I told you time travel was possible. I managed to time travel to the 1940's, during the Second World War London."

Grandpa was so excited about his mission that he just kept talking about his adventure.

Danny laughed and said,

"The black hole adventure was the best roller coaster ride ever. What made me laugh was that Grandpa was singing Beetle songs to all the people at the tube station."

Uncle Phil said,

"Their mission to save Christmas was a success too. This was due to the bravery of Danny."

They all cheered.

Danny felt proud,

"You are right Granddad. Never give up, no matter how bad things get."

Loveness revved the motors and Grandpa contacted Grandma. She appeared on the big screen.

Grandpa blew her a kiss.

"Space Pirates are on their way for a family Christmas."

Grandma blew a kiss back.

"I Love my wonderful family. Can Loveness get me some milk, as Danny will be drinking a lot of hot chocolate from now on?"

All the Space Pirates laughed.

Published in 2024 by FeedARead Publishing

British Library C.I.P.

A CIP catalogue record for this title is available from the British Library.

Printed in Great Britain
by Amazon

46921905R00148